1993

DYNAMICS OF
SUCCESSFUL INTERNATIONAL BUSINESS NEGOTIATIONS

THE MCD SERIES
MANAGING CULTURAL DIFFERENCES

Series Editors: Philip R. Harris, Ph.D. and Robert T. Moran, Ph.D.

◆

DYNAMICS OF
SUCCESSFUL
INTERNATIONAL
BUSINESS
NEGOTIATIONS

Robert T. Moran
William G. Stripp

Gulf Publishing Company
Houston, London, Paris, Zurich, Tokyo

· · · · · · · · ·

We dedicate this book to our wives, Pamela Davis and Virgilia Moran, to our children, and to all of those who are working to become "world class" negotiators.

· · · · · · · · · ·

Managing Cultural Differences Series

Dynamics of
Successful International Business Negotiations

—————◆—————

Gulf Publishing Company
Book Division
P.O. Box 2608, Houston, Texas 77252-2608

10   9   8   7   6   5   4   3   2   1

Library of Congress Cataloging-in-Publication Data

Moran, Robert T., 1948–
        Dynamics of successful international business negotiations /
    Robert T. Moran, William G. Stripp.
            p. cm.—(Managing cultural differences series for international
    business development)
        Includes bibliographical references and index.
        ISBN 0-87201-196-8
        1. International business enterprises—Management.
        2. Negotiation in business.   I. Stripp, William G.   II. Title.
    III. Series.
    HD62.4.M66   1991
    658.4—dc20   90-22306
                                                                              CIP

Contents

Unit I—The Globalization of Business

v

Unit II—The Concept of Culture

Unit III—Global Negotiation

Unit IV—Negotiating with Specific Countries

Acknowledgments

All human beings are walking, talking libraries of diverse experiences. In our conversations with these human libraries and in our observations of their negotiations, we have witnessed the Hegelian dialectic of thesis versus antithesis and the resulting synthesis. What else can one expect when the human libraries' philosophy sections put Karl Marx in touch with Adam Smith, when the religion sections place the Holy Koran next to the Upanishads, when the language sections translate Spanish into Bengali, or when the pure science sections merge nuclear fission with acupuncture. It is like listening to tribes of birds singing back and forth to each other. Sometimes the birdsong amounts to a sweet warbling, at others a horrendous squawking.

In a world of professional confidences and privileged information, it is impossible to acknowledge all of the human libraries who have shared their negotiating successes and failures with us. However, there are certain individuals to whom we would like to give special thanks.

As always, our wives Pamela Davis and Virgilia Moran have been an inspiration and instrumental to our success.

The Gulf editing team has been fantastic and we would like to thank William J. Lowe and Joyce M. Alff for their valuable contributions.

We would also like to thank John C. Condon, Robert A. Lenberg, Noel H. Pugach, Fernando Robles, Robert F. Stripp, Guy Watson, and Lothar Winter for their input and support in developing the first part of the book.

In researching the culture specific material in the second part of the book, we wish to thank Lisa Oplinger, I. Deletang, Sherry Tousley, Eva Vase, Himanshu Mehta, Joseph Petersen, Victor Garcia, Mary Schuler, Anke Esslinger, Jean MacDonald, Francis O'Donnell, Amy Barone, Ron Kornish, and Nancy Decker.

Robert T. Moran
William G. Stripp

Preface

· · · · · · · · ·

International business consultants are faced with an ever present dilemma. Their advice on operating in the international arena is based on an infinite series of assumptions about the nature of the real world. However, these assumptions may prove to be false. What is assumed to be possible often is in fact impossible. What is expected to happen, does not happen. What does happen is unexpected. By the time the truth is determined, the client may incur substantial losses.

Sometimes, however, the consultant's assumptions are correct. For more than thirty years consultants have been warning American businesspeople that world trade and investment is crucial to survival. In "Realities of Our World Position" (*Harvard Business Review* May–June 1959) Peter Drucker wrote that American public and business policies reflected mistaken assumptions about America's position in the world economy.

According to Drucker, American assumptions in 1959 could be simplified into four statements:

- The domestic market is the most important market for the American economy.
- American superiority in productivity and in technological and managerial knowledge is "normal."
- The "dollar gap" is a permanent fixture of the international economy, because foreign countries want as many American goods as they can get and they want much more from America than America shall ever want from them.
- Altogether, the world economy needs America much more than America needs the world economy.

Drucker wrote that reality was much different from what Americans assumed:

- The foreign market is fast becoming the truly critical market for the American economy.
- American leadership in productivity and in technological and managerial know-how is "abnormal," not normal. U.S. leadership is based on temporary factors resulting from other countries' weaknesses, not American strengths.
- The central problem of U.S. economic policy may well become earning enough foreign exchange to pay for its imports.
- America's position in the world economy is both crucial and precarious.

Drucker warned that Americans must realize that leadership is not theirs by right, but must be earned. He further advised that Americans must accept the fact that they were going to be increasingly dependent on the world economy, while the world economy was likely to be less dependent on the United States.

In hindsight it is clear that Drucker was correct. The survival of American business requires increased involvement in world trade and investment. To meet that challenge Americans must understand what "going global" means and how it is done.

In this book we attempt to explain what globalization entails and to provide an overview for developing global strategy and opportunities through effective cross-cultural negotiations.

Our approach will be *behavioral* in the sense that we will attempt to explain behavioral differences in negotiators as a function of cultural influences. The assumption is that a negotiator's attitudes, values, beliefs, and needs are determined at least in part by his or her culture. Negotiating practices and theories will, therefore, vary from culture to culture. Taking the behavioral approach allows us to respond to the question: What are the determinants of human behavior? Or, how can I understand why a negotiator is acting in a particular way?

In the global manager's attempt to understand himself, as well as to comprehend and predict the behavior of others, he or she uses a multilayered frame of explanation. If one knows the culture of the other person, then it is possible to make tentative predictions about the person's behavior. Furthermore, if one knows the other person's social roles and personality; one can predict behavior with a greater degree of accuracy.

Combining our many years of experience, we have collaborated to produce a book that recognizes cross-cultural understanding as a tool for effective international problem solving. It is intended to be of practical use to professional business negotiators, businesspeople who would like to globalize but are unsure how to proceed, students of international business, and academics. We are confident that this book presents techniques to meet the challenge of survival in world trade and investment.

Robert T. Moran
William G. Stripp

1

·········

GOING GLOBAL

The Romance of World Trade

Most businesspeople want to "go global." Why? For some of them going global is a fantasy. It's glamorous. It's sexy. It involves travel to exotic places where exciting adventures and foreign intrigue await. It's like being in a James Bond movie.

Unfortunately, being James Bond can be scary. After all, how many people can hang-glide down onto a moving car, wrestle with a bad guy through the windshield, and then parachute away as the car goes over a cliff? A struggle with a foreign competitor may result in the investment going over the cliff. So businesspeople who are infatuated with globalization for the sexy, superficial reasons generally don't ever globalize. They're like kids looking into a candy shop, fantasizing about the possible delights, but never taking any steps to get what they want. The problem with the candy shop philosophy is that businesspeople lose before they ever start. Fantasies alone will not get them involved in world trade and finance.

However, negotiating on a global scale can present tremendous opportunities. The Global Marketplace can provide corporations with more customers, increased profits, and a longer product/

service life cycle. The Global Factory can provide lower costs, increased productivity, and access to foreign technology. The Global Money Market can provide venture capital, diminished risk, and tax advantages.

Why Globalize? Survival!

The Global Marketplace Provides:
- Larger Profits
- Additional Income on Existing Technology
- Additional Markets
- An Increased Product/Service Life Cycle
- An Opportunity to Offset Lack of Demand for Seasonal Products
- An Opportunity to Gain an Edge in Reputation and Credibility
- A Path to Follow Domestic Customers Who Are "Going Global"
- An Arena to Fight Foreign Competition on a Broader Front
- An Opportunity to Keep Up With Domestic Competitors

The Global Factory Provides:
- Economies of Scale in Production, Logistics, and Marketing
- An Opportunity to Flatten the Learning Curve
- Increased Productivity/Lower Prices
- Additional Product/Service Lines
- Access to Foreign Technology
- Access to Foreign Skill and Knowledge
- Access to Natural Resources
- Better Utilization of Company Personnel

The Global Money Market Provides:
- Access to Foreign Capital
- An Opportunity to Diversify Risk
- An Opportunity to Profit from Foreign Exchange Fluctuations
- Tax Advantages
- A Chance to Escape Close and Unfriendly Government Scrutiny

---

From Domestic to Global and Beyond

The transition from domestic to global corporation may be described as an evolution in four stages: (1) internationalization, (2) multinationalization, (3) transnationalization, and (4) globalization. Beyond globalization are new forms of business that can only be conjectured [26].

What Is Internationalization?

Internationalization is the process by which domestic firms gradually increase international involvement. Beginning with a base in the country of origin, the company slowly goes through a series of independent stages of geographical expansion, each ranked in terms of incremental risk [13, 27, 20].

As Figure 1-1 illustrates, the firm becomes international as it climbs higher on a ladder of strategic foreign market entry choices [31].

A domestic firm's first international experience is usually exporting or licensing. After this initial experience, most firms do not immediately climb further up the internationalization ladder. Instead, international expansion creeps along as the firm slowly increases its knowledge of foreign markets and international operations through interaction with foreign counterparts. Language difficulties and cultural differences pose a major barrier to acquiring knowledge of new opportunities [13].

When a domestic firm begins the internationalization process, it becomes an international business, which means it is involved in direct and indirect exporting, licensing, franchising, manufacturer's contracts, technical agreements, turnkey operations, and joint ventures [25].

Definitions of an International Company include:

• A business involving two or more nations [8].
• A generic term denoting enterprises with various degrees of world-oriented business. The international company engages in any activity or combination of activities from

(continued on next page)

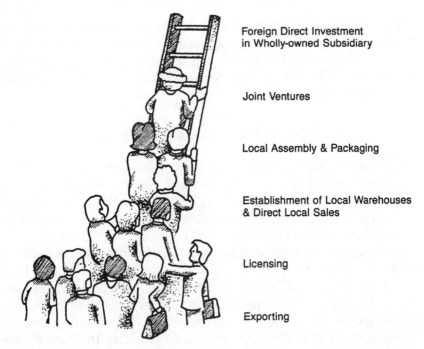

Figure 1-1. *Internationalization: A ladder of strategic foreign market entry choices.*

(continued)
exporting-importing and licensing to full-scale manufacturing in a number of countries [7].
• A firm engaging in foreign business but having no direct foreign investments [24].

A business remains categorized as international until it begins to invest directly in wholly-owned foreign subsidiaries. At some point after the subsidiaries are built, a business becomes multinational.

What Is Multinationalization?

Multinationalization occurs at some point after an international firm begins to make direct investments in wholly-owned foreign subsidiaries. Exactly at what point an international business becomes a multinational corporation (MNC) is debatable. Scholars and consultants use various criteria to distinguish multinational corporations from domestic and international corporations, including [1]:

- Overseas Sales or Earnings
- Location of Foreign Operations
- Overseas Assets
- Number of Foreign Operations
- Management Orientations
- Organizational Structure
- Nationality of Top Management
- Ownership

Normally, before categorizing a firm as multinational some threshold number of foreign operations is required.

The most frequent reason for multinationalization has been to overcome foreign barriers to exports. Business firms also become multinational to adapt their products to local demands, avoid high storage and transportation costs, monitor foreign technological developments, borrow at low interest rates, and reduce total corporate tax liabilities [22 and 11].

Definitions of a Multinational Corporation include:

- A firm that has more than six foreign manufacturing facilities [33].
- A corporation that conducts business in two or more countries in such volume that well-being and growth rest in more than one country and management must make decisions on the basis of multinational alternatives [30].
- A non-financial enterprise with a base of operations in one country and more or less integrated producing-servicing subsidiaries located in several foreign nations [28].
- A manufacturing company that does business in several countries: it has a substantial commitment to its resources in

(continued on next page)

(continued)

international business, it engages in international production in a number of countries, and it has a worldwide perspective in its management [7].

- A conglomerate of autonomous individual country subsidiaries in which manufacturing is only for the country in which production occurs [29].
- A multinational firm that allocates company resources without regard to national frontiers but is nationally based in terms of ownership and top management [24].
- A company that seeks to operate strategically on a global scale [3].
- Any firm that performs its main operations in at least two countries [2].
- A firm that owns income-generating assets in more than one country. To qualify for this label, however, most authorities agree a company should operate in six or more countries and its business should be important enough to influence its overall politics and actions. In practice, multinationals whose annual sales are less than one billion dollars can be ignored [18].
- A company that views each of its businesses around the world as an independent entity, pretty much on its own in serving the national market where it is situated [14].
- A corporation that operates in several countries and adjusts its products and practices in each—at high relative costs [16].

The nature of a firm's industry is a key factor in the decision to become multinational. Multinationalization is most appropriate in industries that are "multi-domestic" or "country-based" by nature. Typically, a business in a multi-domestic industry faces a heterogeneous environment, lacks economies of scale, produces products that differ greatly among country markets, must pay high transportation costs, and does not have great internal resources. Examples of multi-domestic industries include retailing, consumer goods, hazardous chemicals, and metal fabrication [10 and 22].

Strategically, the multinational company competes with other multi-nationals and local competitors on a market-by-market basis. Each individual subsidiary competes in its home country as an essentially autonomous operation. Control is largely decentralized and the subsidiary is expected to make decisions on local research and development, production, marketing, and distribution. The success of the subsidiary as one of the multinational's profit centers is measured by comparing actual versus expected earnings and growth [10].

While much control is decentralized, the MNC has a fiduciary duty to its stockholders to adequately supervise the performance of corporate assets. In meeting this duty, the multinational headquarters must coordinate worldwide financial controls. In effect, the MNC manages a portfolio of foreign investments; however, unlike the usual portfolio of investment securities, this portfolio is made up of actual physical assets [9 and 11].

What Is Transnationalization?

Transnationalization is an advanced stage of multinationalization in which individuals from the branch countries acquire partial ownership of the MNC. While multinational corporations are nationally owned and managed, transnational enterprises (TNEs) are internationally owned and controlled. Some scholars mistakenly equate TNEs with MNCs.

Definitions of a Transnational Corporation include:

- A firm whose ownership and control are both international [28].
- A multinational firm managed and owned by persons of different nationalities [24].
- A firm in which member loyalty transcends national identity, thus eliminating covert or psychologically based national bias in decision making and making possible an optimum allocation of corporate resources insofar as the impact of national law on corporate decisions permits [23].
- Enterprises that own or control production or service facilities outside the country in which they are based [15].

Transnationalization can almost be seen as a denationalization of corporate workers and management. National identity is transcended, thus eliminating home country bias in decision making [22]. Scholars have questioned whether denationalization of business is desirable for host societies and cultures [15, 23].

What Is Globalization?

Globalization occurs when the corporation develops a coordinated system that searches the world to borrow money at the lowest interest rates, purchases resources at the lowest price, manufactures components at the lowest cost, sells goods at the highest profit, and invests returns for the highest gain. The global corporation operates as if the entire world were a single entity. It emphasizes global operations over the domestic market. It selects the best people available for management, regardless of nationality. It locates corporate headquarters anywhere in the world [19, 17, and 14].

Mission Statement for Globalization

- We will search the globe for the best opportunities available.
- We will place our investments around the world to achieve the highest return at the least risk.
- We will purchase raw materials, partially processed items or manufactured items wherever in the world we can do so most economically.
- We will produce either the components or the finished product wherever we can do so most productively.
- We will market our manufactured products wherever we can do so most profitably.
- We will conduct a worldwide search in recruiting our personnel.
- We will conduct our research and development wherever we can capitalize at optimum cost on the technical capabilities that exist in the world.

Definitions of a Global Corporation include:

- An international corporation with global perspective, where domestic operations only exist as an integral part of global operations that are integrated across borders [29].
- A firm that uses economic (or other) advantages to compete in a coordinated way in many national markets [22].
- An enterprise that sells a fairly uniform product in markets all over the earth, and coordinates its international activities accordingly. It may buy components on three continents, ship them to a country with cheap labor to be partially assembled, and then add the finishing touches in factories close to the consumer [14].
- A company that (1) enters markets throughout the world by establishing its own sales and production subsidiaries in several countries and by using other entry modes, (2) exercises control over its subsidiaries, and (3) strives to design and execute corporate strategies in marketing, production, finance, and other functions from a global perspective that transcends national and regional boundaries. A global enterprise is commonly called a multinational or transnational enterprise [25].
- Firms with a third or more of their sales in foreign markets [5].
- An organization that pits its entire worldwide system of product and market position against the competition. The global company—whatever its nationality—tries to control leverage points from cross-national production scale economies to the foreign competitor's sources of cash flow [10].
- A corporation that operates with resolute constancy—at low relative cost—as if the entire world (or major regions of it) were a single entity; it sells the same things in the same way everywhere [16].
- A corporation—or transnational corporation—that looks at the whole world as one market. It manufactures, conducts research, raises capital, and buys supplies wherever it can do the job best. It keeps in touch with technology and market

(continued on next page)

> *(continued)*
> trends all around the world. National boundaries and regula-
> tions tend to be irrelevant, or a mere hindrance. Corporate
> headquarters might be anywhere [19].

The nature of a firm's industry is a key factor in the decision to become global. Globalization is most appropriate for industries that can gain significant benefits from worldwide volume in terms of reduced unit costs or increased reputation. Examples of such industries include automobiles, steel, chemicals, petroleum, cement, agricultural commodities and equipment, industrial and commercial construction, banking and insurance services, computers, semiconductors, publishing, transport, electronic instruments, pharmaceuticals, and telecommunications [16 and 22].

Strategically, the global manufacturer cuts costs and increases price competitiveness by developing a worldwide production configuration that maximizes comparative advantage and economies of scale. The global enterprise "rationalizes" its operations by creating an optimal synergetic mix in which each individual subsidiary specializes in a part of production. For example, components may be produced in subsidiaries close to sources of raw materials and shipped for assembly in subsidiaries where labor is cheapest [10 and 14].

The global marketeer bases the firm's marketing strategy on a few standardized world markets rather than on many customized markets. The corporation offers globally standardized products that are advanced, functional, reliable, and, above all, relatively low-priced. The global corporation doesn't completely reject product customization and differentiation, but adjusts to differences in product preferences only after exhausting all efforts to retain standardization [16].

Multinationalization Versus Globalization

The philosophies of multinationalization and globalization are based upon fundamentally different assumptions about the nature of the modern world. The multinationalists see a heterogeneous world where transportation and storage costs are high, technology is rapidly changing, governmental restrictions are severe, and product needs and preferences are diverse. To compete in such a world the multinational corporation manages a portfolio of independent positions. The MNC evaluates each market as an independent entity and pursues high-profit markets more aggressively than low-profit markets [10 and 22].

The globalists see a homogenous world where technological advances have reduced transportation and communications costs, softened governmental constraints, and narrowed national economic and social differences. To compete in such a world the global corporation must take advantage of economies of scale to reduce costs and price. The focus on worldwide volume enables the global corporation to enter low-profit markets [10]. (See Table 1-1.)

Table 1-1
Factors in Choosing a Strategy of
Multinationalization or Globalization

	Multinationalize if:	Globalize if:
Environment is:	heterogeneous	homogeneous
Scale economies are:	low	high
Type of product is:	customized	standardized
Transport costs are:	high	low
Company resources are:	low	high

Future Forms of International Corporations

The most successful future businesses may be small or medium-sized companies rather than giant corporations. Computer-aided design, manufacturing and engineering (CAD/CAM/CAE), robotics, and new equipment and process technology (EPT) may make small "transnational confederations" as efficient as large global corporations. Transnational confederations will be located close to their markets and will use "economies of scope" to produce great varieties of relatively customized products at remarkably low prices [16 and 6].

The characteristics of transnational confederations are:

- A small or medium-sized company, rather than a large company.
- Managers lead an orchestra, rather than an army.
- Politically invisible, rather than politically active.
- Composed of two companies: one that designs and markets products worldwide and one that manufactures products.
- Primarily a managing or marketing company, rather than a manufacturing company.
- Control through marketing, rather than legal authority.
- Cohesion through control of marketing, rather than control of capital.
- Many stages of production performed by subcontractors, rather than subsidiaries or branches.
- Production operations not labor intensive.
- Primarily organized around technology, design, and marketing.
- Production operations rely on CAD/CAE/CAM, robotics, and EPT.

At some time in the future, international political organizations such as the United Nations may reach agreements that enable businesses to trade free from government restrictions. A "supranational firm" would be a transnational firm that is legally denationalized by becoming incorporated through an international agency [24].

If businesses are freed from international political constraints, they may be able to act as leaders in a movement toward a more fully-integrated world. The primary role for the "world corporation" will be the coordination of a transcultural, total mankind-oriented approach to shaping the system of human living. The world corporation will link governments, businesses, and universities to marshall the resources of science and technology to redesign society's systems [12].

The evolution of international businesses from simple export-trading companies into world organizations may spur the development of "transideological institutions" that neutralize destructive competitiveness among nation-states by working for the common good of mankind [21].

The evolution of the international corporation might proceed as follows:

International Corporation
  Multinational Corporation
    Transnational Corporation
      Global Corporation
        Transnational Confederation
          Supranational Firm
            World Organization
              Transideological Institution

Summary

While world trade and investment seem glamorous and exciting, the most important reason for globalization is survival. The transition from domestic to global corporation may be thought of as an evolutionary process. A business becomes international when it moves out of the domestic market. International businesses are involved in activities ranging from exporting to joint ventures. A business becomes multinational when it begins to make direct investments in several wholly owned foreign subsidiaries. Transnationalization occurs when partial ownership and control of the multinational corporation is acquired by individuals from the branch countries. A corporation is global when it becomes a fully integrated system, operating as if the entire world were a single entity.

References and Suggested Readings

1. Aharoni, Yair. "On the Definition of a Multinational Corporation." *Quarterly Review of Economics and Business*, Autumn 1971.

2. Brooke, Michael Z. and H.L. Remmers. *The Strategy of Multinational Enterprise.* New York: American Elsevier, 1970.
3. Channon, Derek F. with M. Jalland. *Multinational Strategic Planning.* New York: AMACOM, 1978.
4. Clee, Gilbert H. and A. diScipio. "Creating a World Enterprise." *Harvard Business Review,* November–December 1959, pp. 77–89.
5. Davidson, Richard H. *Global Strategic Management.* New York: John Wiley & Sons, 1982.
6. Drucker, Peter F. *Managing in Turbulent Times.* New York: Harper & Row, 1980.
7. Dymsza, William A. *Multinational Business Strategy.* New York: McGraw-Hill Book Company, 1972.
8. Fayerweather, John. *International Business Management: A Conceptual Framework.* New York: McGraw-Hill Book Co., 1969.
9. ———. "Four Winning Strategies for the International Corporation." *Journal of Business Strategy,* Fall Vol. 2, 1981.
10. Hout, Thomas, M.E. Porter and E. Rudden. "How Global Companies Win Out." *Harvard Business Review.* Sept.–Oct. 1982, pp. 98+.
11. Jacoby, Neil H. "The Multinational Corporation." *The Center Magazine,* Vol. 3, No. 1, May 1970.
12. Jantsch, Erich. "The 'World Corporation': The Total Commitment." *Columbia Journal of World Business,* May–June 1971, pp. 5–12.
13. Johanson, J. and J. Vahlne. "The Internationalization Process of the Firm." *Journal of International Business Studies,* Spring/Summer 1977, pp. 23–32.
14. Kiechel, Walter. "Playing the Global Game." *Fortune,* November 18, 1981, pp. 111+.
15. Kumar, Krishna. *The Social and Cultural Impacts of Transnational Enterprises.* Sydney, Australia: University of Sydney, 1979.
16. Levitt, Theodore. "The Globalization of Markets." *Harvard Business Review,* May–June 1983, pp. 92.
17. Linfield, Seymour L. "Looking Around: Overseas Operations." *Harvard Business Review,* September–October 1960, pp. 41–46.

18. Madsen, Axel. *Private Power.* New York: William Morrow and Company, 1980.
19. Main, Jeremy. "How to Go Global—And Why." *Fortune,* August 28, 1989, pp. 70+.
20. Newbould, Gerald D., P. Buckley, & J. Thurwell. *Going International: The Experience of Smaller Companies Overseas.* New York: John Wiley & Sons, 1978.
21. Perlmutter, Howard V. "Toward Research on and Development of Nations, Unions, and Firms as Worldwide Institutions." Paper presented at Symposium on Collective Bargaining, *International Institute for Labour Studies.* Geneva, 1969.
22. Porter, Michael E. *Competitive Strategy.* New York: Free Press, 1980.
23. Robinson, Richard D. *International Business Management.* Hinsdale, Illinois: The Dryden Press, 1978.
24. Robock, Stefan H. and K. Simmonds. *International Business and Multinational Enterprises.* Homewood, Illinois: Richard D. Irwin, Inc., 1973.
25. Root, Franklin R. *Foreign Market Entry Strategies.* New York: AMACOM, 1982.
26. ———. *Entry Strategies for Foreign Markets: From Domestic to International Business.* New York: AMACOM, 1977.
27. Rugman, Alan M. "A New Theory of the Multinational Enterprise: Internationalization versus Internalization."*Columbia Journal of World Business,* Spring 1980, pp. 23–29.
28. Salera, Virgil. *Multinational Business.* Boston: Houghton Mifflin Company, 1969.
29. Schwendiman, John S. *Strategic and Long-Range Planning for the Multinational Corporation.* New York: Praeger, 1973.
30. Steiner, George S. and W. Cannon. *Multinational Corporate Planning.* New York: The Macmillan Company, 1966.
31. Steinmann, H., B. Kumar, and A. Wasner. "Internationalisierungsstrategien von Mittelbetrieben." *Schriften zur Unternehmensfuhrung,* Vol. 25, 1978.
32. ———. "Conceptualizing the Internationalization Process of Medium Sized Firms." *Management International Review,* 20(1), pp. 50–66.
33. Vernon, Raymond. *Sovereignty at Bay.* New York: Basic Books, 1971.

2

·········

HOW TO GO GLOBAL

Developing a Strategy

The most important reason for globalization is survival. The survival of a corporation in the modern world depends upon having an effective strategy. "Strategy" can be defined as the art and science of controlling and using the resources of a business unit or a coalition of business units to effectively promote and secure the vital interests of the enterprise. While the general principles of strategy are immutable, scholars have differentiated between "international," "multinational," "regional," and "global" business strategy [10, 24].

"International strategy" is a composite of several individual foreign market entry plans. An entry strategy is needed for each product in each foreign market. The firm must choose (1) a target market, (2) the objectives in the market, (3) an entry mode to penetrate the market, (4) the marketing plan to enter the target market, and (5) the control system to monitor performance [21].

Definitions of international strategy include:

• A plan to control a firm's destiny through the efficient use of its business opportunities and resources [2].

(continued on next page)

16

(continued)
- A comprehensive plan for entry in foreign markets that sets objectives, goals, resources, and policies for a long enough period to sustain growth in world markets [21].

"Multinational strategy" is based upon portfolio planning theory. The multinational strategist evaluates individual markets on a stand-alone basis. He assesses the strengths and weaknesses of existing and potential subsidiaries through managerial audits and evaluates threats and opportunities in existing and potential markets through environmental profiles. He then ranks each market in terms of potential profitability and growth [11].

The multinational corporation (MNC) aggressively pursues entry into high-profit or high-growth markets. Following portfolio planning theory, the MNC allocates corporate resources on the basis of potential profitability and growth of individual markets. If a market appears to be strong, the MNC aggressively defends it. If a market appears weak, the MNC either tries to turn it around using minimal resources or abandons the market completely [11 and 5].

Definitions of multinational strategy include:

- A systematic way of dealing with the opportunities, risks, and problems that are important to a multinational company's future over an extended period of time [5].
- A twofold plan to identify the strategic options most relevant to the corporation and to narrow down these options into the one best plan [13].
- A plan to (a) determine major goals for the enterprise as a whole as well as for its subsidiaries, and (b) adopt essential courses of action in terms of policies, programs, and action plans throughout the enterprise to achieve the predetermined goals [19].

"Regional strategy" involves regional strongholds that concentrate on markets within the region's sphere of influence. The corporation is highly interdependent on a regional basis. Regional headquarters control local subsidiaries and collaborate with other regions to attain broad objectives [9].

"Triad power" is a form of regional strategy that centers around three main regions: Japan, the United States, and Europe. Besides interacting within the triad, each multiregional company creates a "tetrahedron" by influencing developing areas immediately to its geographic south. Other regions are less important for survival and can be treated as marginal and/or opportunistic [17].

Japanese triad power is operative primarily in the United States, Europe, and Asia. American triad power is exercised over Japan, Europe, and Latin America. European triad power is exercised over the United States, Japan, and Africa and/or the Middle East. Each triad power must become truly knowledgeable of and accepted within its region.

What Is a Multiregional Company?

A multiregional company (MRC) can be viewed as a natural step in the evolution of the multinational company in that headquarters recognizes the commonalities of the regions and the uniqueness of the key marketplaces. As such, regional headquarters are formed to complement each other across the tetrahedron and to allocate and use global resources against key competitive threats. Common functions are shared in the regions and across the regions to gain synergistic advantage over competitor's quality and cost position [17].

"Global strategy" is an integrated system for dealing with corporate opportunities and threats on a worldwide basis. The global strategist coordinates a worldwide system of market positions, facilities, and investments, and focuses on leveraging positions in one country's market against those in other markets. For example, the global enterprise may establish blocking positions in nations where rivals are attempting to set up a base for global competition. By undercutting the competitor's price, the global enterprise can prevent the competitor from getting the cash flow necessary to go global.

Definitions of global strategy include:

- A process or integrated system for dealing with worldwide corporate challenges, opportunities, and problems [22].
- A plan whereby an enterprise makes major business decisions based on global opportunities, global alternatives, and future global consequences. The decision maker frees himself of any national blinders and considers world markets and world-resource locations instead of the markets or resources of a particular country in isolation. The aim is to achieve maximum results on a multinational basis rather than to treat international activities as a portfolio of diverse and separate country companies. Generally the enterprise engages in a formal process of strategic and long-range planning [20].
- A process of defining, developing and administering a strategy and structure for a worldwide business [3].
- A process whereby an organization no longer views its international operation as a collection of diverse foreign subsidiaries but instead develops a strategy that attempts to maximize results from the firm's total operation. Top management must view the world as a total market with a total source of input and select a strategy designed to maximize the output from the world [1].

Framework for Developing a Strategy

Strategy comprises general principles that have remained constant throughout history and are universally applicable. Business strategy always involves long-term planning; defining business objectives; analyzing one's own and the competitor's strength; understanding the geography of the land and planning moves accordingly; assessing options and preparing contingency plans; organizing transport, supplies, and communication; anticipating the competitor's actions; and determining when and where to do business [24].

The general principles of strategy always include a central purpose, a set of objectives, an intelligence function with emphasis on analysis of internal and external strengths and weaknesses, a consideration of alternative actions, a strategic choice, and a means of coordination and control. Strategy considers the whole picture, determining when and where to act. Logistics organizes the internal resources and develops the lines of communication, supply, reinforcement, and retreat. Tactics occur at contact and determine the manner of execution and employment of resources. All of this is driven by policy that is an outgrowth of individual and group philosophy.

The framework for developing corporate strategy is the same whether an enterprise wishes to expand internationally, multinationally, regionally, or globally. It is up to each enterprise to use the framework to develop a plan that fits its philosophy and objectives.

Framework for Developing a Global Strategy

1. General Philosophy: What is the firm's basic reason for existence?

2. Analysis and Diagnosis:
   External: Do opportunities exist outside the domestic environment which can benefit the firm?
   Internal: Can the firm meet global opportunities if they are present?

3. Mission Statement: Given the results of the analysis and diagnosis, what is the firm's vision for its future existence as a global enterprise?

4. Objectives: Within a specified time period, what outcomes does the firm desire to achieve?

5. Strategic Alternatives: How can the firm take advantage of the available global opportunities while avoiding global threats?

(continued on next page)

(continued)

6. Strategic Choice:	Which alternative is most appropriate to the firm's situation?
7. Contingency Plan:	Given the possibility of failing, which alternative should the firm fall back upon?
8. Implementation:	
Leadership:	Who will be selected to implement the global strategy?
Personnel:	How will personnel be chosen?
Logistics:	How will the lines of global communication and supply be organized?
Tactics:	How will global resources be deployed?
9. Evaluation:	How does the firm know if its plan is working?

Strategic Alternatives

Corporations consider international strategic alternatives every day, such as whether or not to borrow money from a foreign bank, or whether or not to purchase foreign supplies. While these decisions seem simple, they are the first steps toward the corporation's becoming an international firm.

It is a small step from making purchases in the global marketplace to exporting indirectly. Contacts are often made socially. A cocktail party might be the scene of a deal struck between a CEO of a domestic corporation and an export merchant who buys local products and sells them in other countries.

As a corporation gains initiative, it may approach an export agent to act as its representative overseas or an export management company to develop export sales. For some companies, the best exporting method may be to "piggyback" by selling products to a local company whose products are already well-placed on the international market.

Other firms are content to wait for contact from a commission buying agent hired by a foreign importer to find and buy products at a low price.

If a corporation wants to retain greater control over its foreign marketing plan or receive quicker feedback from foreign customers, it might want to export directly. To do this, it can approach a foreign sales agent to sell its product on a commission basis. Alternatively, a corporation might decide to sell to a foreign distributor who will resell to other middlemen or final buyers, or it might decide to sell directly to the foreign consumer [23].

Once a corporation begins to feel comfortable overseas, it may decide to establish a foreign warehouse to store its product or a foreign branch sales office to sell the product. It might become involved in international barter or other forms of countertrade to increase its profit potential or to overcome foreign exchange restrictions. It might even be approached to become involved in a cross-distribution agreement, in which it distributes a foreign company's goods on the domestic market while the foreign company distributes its goods on the foreign market.

If a corporation has intangible assets, such as patents, trade secrets, know-how, trademarks, or a prestigious company name, it might choose to become involved in various forms of licensing. Licensing enables a foreign company to produce and manufacture a product without the equity participation or management control of the licensor. A corporation also might choose to franchise its business system, permitting the foreign franchisee to do business under its name and training the franchisee to follow set policies and procedures. If this method is unsatisfactory, it might enter a management contract or a technical-assistance contract to provide professional services to the foreign corporation.

A corporation can enter contract manufacturing agreements to transfer technology and assistance to a foreign manufacturer, buy the manufactured product, and sell it in the foreign market or elsewhere. Or a corporation might enter a turnkey construction contract to build a manufacturing operation overseas for a foreign buyer.

At some point a corporation may decide to invest directly in foreign production to obtain raw materials, acquire manufactured products at a lower cost, or penetrate local markets. The direct investment may be a joint venture with a foreign company in which both act as partners and share the equity. Joint ventures are often mandated by local law or necessitated by inexperience in the foreign market. Sometimes several corporations will become involved in a complex joint venture referred to as a consortium.

If a corporation desires greater control and flexibility in pricing and dividend policy, it may choose to acquire complete ownership of foreign branch plants or subsidiaries. As the firm matures, it may choose to sell equity securities in its branch plant to foreign investors and managers. Further down the road, it may decide to rationalize its operations and limit production in its branches to specific components. Manufacturing may be drastically curtailed and the corporation might rely on outsourcing agreements to obtain needed parts.

Perhaps the corporation will leave production altogether and limit itself to management and service functions. It may create a research consortium with other mature firms. Acting out of the research consortium, the firm could limit its activities to technology transfer or R&D exchanges.

The corporation should choose a global mix of foreign entry strategies that is appropriate to its policy and internal resources [21]. Firms with absolutely no international experience would be wise to consider a strategic alliance with an experienced partner.

Strategic Alternatives in World Trade and Investment

- Strategic Alliances
- Transnational Ownership of Equity Securities
- Transnational Management Organization
- Wholly Owned Manufacturing Branch Plant or Subsidiaries
- Consortium
- Joint Ventures
- Cross-Production Agreements
- Turnkey Operations
- Manufacturer's Contracts
- Research Consortium
- Outsourcing Agreements

(continued on next page)

- Franchising
- Licensing with Partial Ownership
- Cross-Licensing Agreements
- Licensing
- Management or Technical Assistance Contracts
- Cross-Distribution Agreements
- International Barter & Countertrade
- Foreign Branch Sales Office
- Foreign Warehouse
- Export Directly to the "End User"
  - Directly to a "Foreign Distributor"
  - Directly through a "Foreign Sales Agent"
  - Indirectly through an "Export Management Company"
  - Indirectly by Hiring an "Export Agent"
  - Indirectly by "Piggybacking" on an International Company
  - Indirectly by Selling to an "Export Merchant"
  - Indirectly by Selling to a "Commission Buying Agent"
- Purchasing Foreign Goods
- Obtaining Foreign Capital

Strategic Alliances

Strategic alliances are partnerships between firms that work together under a cooperative agreement to attain some strategic objective. Corporations that want to globalize are often well-advised to enter into an alliance to offset the immense expense that globalization entails. Allies share costs, establish a pool of joint resources, and create a synergistic effect in the problem-solving process [16 and 28].

Definitions of a Strategic Alliance include:

- Global Strategic Partnerships (GSPs) in which: (1) Two or more companies develop a common, long-term strategy

(continued on next page)

(continued)

aimed at world leadership as low-cost suppliers, differentiated marketers, or both, in an international arena. (2) The relationship is reciprocal. The partners possess specific strengths that they are prepared to share with their colleagues. (3) The partners' efforts are global, extending beyond a few developed countries to include nations of the newly industrializing, less developed, and socialist world. (4) The relationship is organized along horizontal, not vertical, lines; technology exchanges, resource pooling, and other "soft" forms of combination are the rule. (5) The participating companies retain their national and ideological identities while competing in those markets excluded from the partnership [18].

- Partnerships, such as joint ventures and cooperative agreements, in which firms work together to attain some strategic objective. "Joint ventures" create a jointly-owned entity, while non-equity forms of cooperation do not [7].
- Co-operative agreements, such as technology swaps; research and development exchanges; distribution, marketing and manufacturer-supplier relationships; and cross-licenses. Such agreements have been widely practiced in most sectors of the economy for a long time [12].
- Diverse forms of cooperative agreements ranging from equity joint ventures and licensing agreements to technology transfers and research and development partnerships to supplier and marketing arrangements [15].
- A variety of business relationships: some temporary, others permanent, some formal, others informal, frequently referred to in business literature as strategic alliances or partnerships.

  Strategic partnerships fall into two categories: (1) firms with contractual agreements formed because of either complementary expertise, successful shared experience, or both; or (2) firms that agree—without contractual agreements— to work together because of complementary expertise, successful shared experience, or both [28].
- Competitive Collaboration including joint ventures, outsourcing agreements, product licensings, and cooperative research [6].

The biggest impetus to alliance formation has been the emergence of global competitors. The rapid pace of technological development and the increasingly high costs of associated research and development are also factors in alliance decisions. Sometimes governments provide a further stimulus, openly encouraging collaboration between certain companies [4].

The goal of strategic partnering is to combine financial, marketing, production, and technological resources in a way that serves common objectives. The partners might want to increase market share, dissuade a competitor from globalizing, increase the flow of innovation, or improve flexibility in responding to market and technological changes [15 and 12].

The success of an alliance depends upon the compatibility of the partners. A company must take the time to find a partner with a cooperative business philosophy, a complementary mission, compatible managerial capabilities, and parallel products based on adaptable technology [15, 7, and 8].

Perhaps the most crucial prerequisite to the success of an alliance is careful selection of the individuals who will represent the individual corporations. The alliance board members must be functionally matched to the mission and be willing to support it. Project managers must be willing to share selected expertise and organizational resources. Team members must be willing to cooperate in joint marketing, sales, and R&D efforts. Generally, there must be total commitment to a true team effort [28].

In developing alliance strategy, the partners must avoid "niche collision." Alliance members may be involved in other partnerships that are conducting business in the same or similar markets. This would put a corporation in the position of both cooperating with and competing against its partners. One partner may charge another with using information gained through the alliance to betray the partnership [18].

To avoid potential losses some commentators suggest that corporations consider alliances as competition in a different form. The objective is to gain a form of strategic synergy where the corporation gains the benefits of cooperation without forgetting that the partner is an actual or potential competitor [6].

Other commentators believe that an alliance must be run like a marriage. Firms must find a dancing partner who can complement the firm's strategy. If the partners marry, they must create a nurturing environment or risk a messy divorce. Offspring of the alliance, such as a joint venture, need as much attention and support as a baby [8].

Alliances face many barriers to success, ranging from antitrust laws to cultural attitudes. One major problem area is the difficulty many firms have in giving up total control. The alliance board must create a clear line of authority. Alliance management must then decide who has access to information, who has the authorization to release plans and specifications, and what gets released from manufacturing [28].

The changing interests of alliance members may create problems. The life of the partnership depends upon the ability of members to sustain their commitment because of mutuality of interest. Partners will leave if they lose interest or the venture appears unsuccessful. A corporation must be sure that a potential partner will remain interested in the alliance or be prepared to go through a costly dissolution [12].

Often the biggest internal struggle in an alliance is the conflict between corporate cultures. As cultural chemistry is seen as the most important factor in the endurance of the alliance, conflicts can be devastating. Cultural incompatibility can lead to complete shutdown of partnership operations. The partners must be willing to create an "alliance culture" while retaining their corporate identities [18].

Corporate survival in an age of alliances does not amount to a survival of the fittest, because corporations need not be the strongest, the shrewdest, or the most dominant. The survivors will be those corporations that cooperate best in the creation of alliances [27, 26, 25, and 18].

Summary

The survival of a global corporation is dependent upon the development of an effective strategy. Global strategy is an integrated system for dealing with corporate opportunities and threats on a worldwide basis.

Corporations have many strategic alternatives for becoming involved in world trade and investment. Opportunities include direct and indirect exporting, countertrade, licensing, franchising, management contracts, turnkey operations, joint ventures, wholly owned subsidiaries, and research consortia. The corporation can choose a global mix of foreign entry strategies that is appropriate to its policy and internal resources.

One of the best strategic alternatives is to become involved in a strategic alliance with an experienced partner. Allies share costs, establish a pool of joint resources, and create a synergistic effect in problem solving. Corporations should make sure that they choose a partner that is culturally compatible.

References and Suggested Readings

1. Bates, David and Donald Eldredge. *Strategy and Policy.* New York: Allyn Publishers, 1984.
2. Brooke, Michael Z. and M. van Beusekom. *International Corporate Planning.* London: Pitman Publishing Limited, 1979.
3. Davidson, Richard H. *Global Strategic Management.* New York: John Wiley & Sons, 1982.
4. Devlin, Godfrey and Mark Bleackley. "Strategic Alliances: Guidelines for Success." *Long Range Planning,* 1988, Vol. 21. No. 5, pp. 18–23.
5. Dymsza, William A. *Multinational Business Strategy.* New York: McGraw-Hill Book Company, 1972.
6. Hamel, Gary, Y. Doz, and C. Prahalad. "Collaborate with Your Competitors and Win." *Harvard Business Review,* January–February 1989, pp. 133–139.
7. Harrigan, K.R. "Strategic Alliances and Partner Asymmetries." *Management International Review,* 1988, pp. 53+.
8. ————. "Strategic Alliances: Their New Role in Global Competition." *Columbia Journal of World Business,* Summer 1987, pp. 67–69.
9. Heenan, David A. and Howard Perlmutter. *Multinational Organization Development: A Social Architectural Perspective.* Reading, Massachusetts: Addison-Wesley Publishing Company, 1979.
10. Holstein, William J. "Going Global." *Business Week,* October 20, 1989, pp. 9–18.
11. Hout, Thomas, M.E. Porter and E. Rudden. "How Global Companies Win Out." *Harvard Business Review.* Sept.–Oct, 1982, pp. 98+.

12. James, Barrie G. "Alliance: The New Strategic Focus." *Long Range Planning*, 1985, Vol. 18. No. 3, pp. 76–81.
13. Lorange, Peter. "A Framework for Strategic Planning in Multinational Corporations." *Long Range Planning*, June 1976.
14. Main, Jeremy. "How to Go Global—And Why." *Fortune*, August 28, 1989, pp. 70+.
15. Modic, Stanley J. "Strategic Alliances." *Industry Week*, October 3, 1988, pp. 46–52.
16. Ohmae, Kenichi. "The Global Logic of Strategic Alliances." *Harvard Business Review*, March–April 1989, pp. 143–154.
17. ———. *Triad Power: The Coming Shape of Global Competition*. New York: The Free Press, 1985.
18. Perlmutter, Howard V. and David A. Heenan. "Cooperate to Compete Globally." *Harvard Business Review*, March–April 1986, pp. 136+.
19. Prasad, S. and K.Y. Shetty. *An Introduction to Multinational Management*. Englewood Cliffs, NJ: Prentice Hall, 1976.
20. Robock, Stefan H. and K. Simmonds. *International Business and Multinational Enterprises*. Homewood, Illinois: Richard D. Irwin, Inc., 1973.
21. Root, Franklin R. *Foreign Market Entry Strategies*. New York: AMACOM, 1982.
22. Schwendiman, John S. *Strategic and Long-Range Planning for the Multinational Corporation*. New York: Praeger, 1973.
23. Small Business Administration. *Export Training Program for SBA Personnel*. Washington, D.C.: SBA, 1980.
24. Stripp, William G. "Sun Tzu, Musashi and Mahan: The Integration of Chinese, Japanese and American Strategic Thought." Paper presented at Inaugural Meeting of the SE Asia Region, *Academy of International Business*. Hong Kong, 1985.
25. Thomas, Lewis. *Late Night Thoughts on Listening to Mahler's Ninth Symphony*. New York: Viking Press, 1983.
26. ———. *The Medusa & the Snail*. New York: Bantam Books, 1979.
27. ———. *The Lives of a Cell: Notes of a Biology Watcher*. New York: Viking Press, 1974.
28. Weimer, George, B. Knill, S. Modic, and C. Potter. "Strategic Alliances make Marketing and Manufacturing an International Game." *Industry Week*, October 3, 1988, pp. IM8–30.

3
......

FINDING GLOBAL OPPORTUNITIES

Global Strategic Intelligence

Global business strategy involves intelligence operations. "Global strategic intelligence" is knowledge of the world environment that the firm needs to accomplish its mission and avoid acting in ignorance. "Environment" means all those factors important to the firm's success and over which it has little or no control. These include the political, economic, legal, social, and cultural contexts in which the firm operates [2, 10, 23].

The firm obtains intelligence through analyzing and projecting key environmental variables. The analysis involves: (1) selection and accumulation of facts relating to global opportunities and threats; (2) evaluation and interpretation of the facts; and, (3) presentation of the facts clearly and meaningfully in oral or written reports [6].

A corporation obtains information about global opportunities and threats through search and surveillance. Search, also known as research, involves prospecting for information to learn from patterns in the past. Unfortunately, global research operations are often complex and expensive, and corporations frequently refrain from using them [9].

Global surveillance operations put the contemporary world under close and systematic observation. Surveillance involves passive watching. Most corporations gather surveillance information in an ad hoc and informal manner, resulting in largely intuitive and individualistic analysis [9].

Some scholars suggest that a firm can do nothing about the subjective nature of global intelligence operations because it is an art that relies upon the personal characteristics of the intelligence analyst. Therefore, the best approach would be to hire good people as intelligence analysts, give them a free rein, let them do their work, and listen to them when they find something out [11, 12].

Good intelligence analysts are difficult to find outside the firm and take a long time to develop inside the firm. As a result, many businesses give up entirely and fail to recognize significant global opportunities and threats. One solution is to rely upon government agencies, banks, or "information boutiques." Information boutiques are intelligence consulting organizations run by former government agents and academics [22].

In evaluating the opportunities in the international environment, businesses should pay particular attention to changing conditions in the Global Money Market, the Global Marketplace, and the Global Factory.

The Global Money Market

Perhaps the most important aspect of the globalization of a domestic firm is access to the Global Money Market in over 100 sovereign nation-states. Each nation has different resources and economic policies, resulting in significant variability in taxation, interest rates, foreign exchange rates, and availability of venture capital. A global enterprise can structure its financial strategy to profit from these differences.

Differences in international tax rates have a strong impact on the location of international operations, the legal form of the new enterprise, the method of corporate financing, and the allocation of costs between corporate business units. Traditionally, firms take advantage of the tax differential through methods such as transfer pricing and cost allocation [17].

Global tax tactics include:

- Intracorporate Pricing/Transfer Pricing
- Cost Allocation
- Dividend Disbursement
- Method of Accounting

By realizing profits in countries with low tax rates and taking advantage of the way a government in one country treats taxes paid in another country, global enterprises realize substantial gains. However, governments often attack such methods, and the firm must defend its tax strategies. Generally, tax law and treaties provide for negotiation of disputes [5].

International securities markets provide global enterprises with an opportunity to invest and raise capital. As Figure 3-1 illustrates,

The Global Stock Market

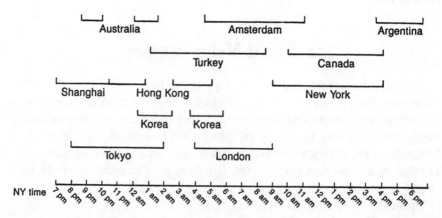

Figure 3-1. *A global enterprise can play the market 24 hours a day by shifting money between stock exchanges.*

rapid advances in technology and deregulation by governments result in a Global Stock Market of approximately four dozen stock exchanges. The Big Three are the Tokyo Stock Exchange (TSE), the New York Stock Exchange (NYSE), and the London Stock Exchange (LSE) [29].

A global enterprise may raise capital by listing its stock on several foreign exchanges. The additional advantage of doing this is to gain exposure to foreign investors who might later be tapped for debt financing. The global enterprise can also invest excess capital by playing the market 24 hours a day and shifting money between four dozen stock exchanges [29].

The five big players in the global stock market are Nomura Securities and Daiwa Securities in Japan, Merrill Lynch & Company and Salomon Inc. in the United States, and Barclays Bank PLC in the United Kingdom. Nikko Securities and Yamaichi Securities of Japan are rapidly catching up. A global enterprise may negotiate with these or other securities firms to disseminate new capital stock or to float a new bond issue.

Rather than diluting equity interest, a global enterprise may obtain financing through the Global Banking Industry. The globalization of banking provides opportunities to take advantage of international differences in the cost of capital. International variability in money supply, political stability, rate of inflation, and governmental monetary policy produce interest rates that are lower in some countries than they are in others. Simply put, a global enterprise can borrow money in countries where interest rates are relatively low and use the money in countries where interest rates are higher. These small differences can provide the global enterprise with tremendous savings [24].

In addition to providing low-interest loans, global banks provide many services including insurance, currency forecasting, and investment banking. This range of services should expand as competition between the global banks increases. Japanese financial strength resulted in great structural changes that shook many major banks out of their complacency. In 1980, Japan had only one bank among the world's ten largest banking companies. In 1990 the world's ten largest banking companies are all Japanese.

The Ten Largest Banks in the World in 1990 are:
- Dai-Ichi Kangyo Bank, Ltd.
- Sumitomo Bank, Ltd.
- Fuji Bank, Ltd.
- Sanwa Bank, Ltd.
- Mitsubishi Bank, Ltd.

- Industrial Bank of Japan
- Norinchukin Bank
- Tokai Bank Ltd.
- Mitsui Bank Ltd.
- Mitsubishi Trust

Presenting Complex Data

In using the Global Money Market, a global enterprise can develop and rely on many creative analytical devices. One of the most creative and humorous is the "Burger Barometer," as illustrated in Figure 3-2. The inspiration for this device was McDonald's global expansion, that is, from McDonald's to McParis to McMoscow to McWorld. The Burger Barometer determines whether or not foreign exchange rates are in line by comparing the price of a Big Mac, a small order of fries, and a glass of Coke at McDonald's all over the world. This is a rather unique way of keeping track of fluctuations in the foreign exchange rate.

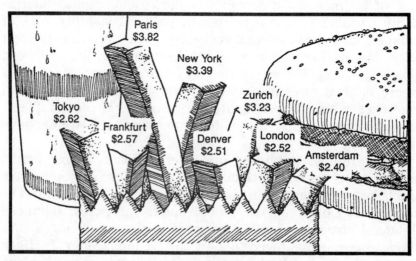

Figure 3-2. "The Burger Barometer" determines whether foreign exchange rates are in line by comparing the price of a Big Mac all over the world.

By using devices such as the Burger Barometer, the international environmental analyst can present complex international financial data in a way that policy makers will understand and appreciate.

The Global Marketplace

From the time of the ancient Phoenicians, businesspeople recognized that profits can be made by playing with comparative cost advantages between countries. Today, the survival of the world depends upon the maintenance of free trade. National survival and growth is often based upon importation of strategic natural resources. Corporate survival would be severely jeopardized if foreign markets were completely closed. Individuals would face a drastic reduction in quality of life if imports were shut off. Many Americans would "just die" if they couldn't keep their German car, Japanese VCR, French cheese, Australian beer, and Swiss chocolate.

Of course, some groups would like to severely restrict or eliminate free trade. Protectionist factions in every national political system call for barriers to foreign goods and investment. Trade barriers include tariffs, subsidies, multiple exchange rates, foreign exchange controls, customs valuations, quotas, "buy local" regulations, discriminatory import licensing, and arbitrary safety and industrial standards [5]. But closed minds at home don't open up markets abroad, and every nation's survival depends upon the continuation of open foreign markets [15].

For corporations, the question is not whether to enter the global marketplace but how to enter it. The long, ongoing debate continues over whether the proper approach to international marketing is a global, standardized approach or a multinational, localized approach. The answer depends upon the match between the firm's resources and the target markets.

International Marketing: Standardized or Localized?

• The exporter must decide whether to conform to local prejudices, or, by salesmanship and educational processes, to overcome them. The latter course means additional sales expenses
(continued on next page)

(continued)

and is rarely completely successful, but it has many advantages for exporters of standard, mass-produced products [7].

- Traditionally, marketing strategy was strictly a local problem in each national market. Differences in customer needs and preferences, in competition, in institutional systems and in legal regulations required different marketing programs. Any similarity between countries was purely coincidental.

Differences among nations are still great and companies should recognize them in marketing planning. But the experiences of many multinational companies suggest that real gains are possible with an integrated approach to marketing strategy. Standardization of products, packages, and promotional approaches may permit substantial cost savings and greater consistency in dealings with customers. Harmonizing price policies often facilitates better internal planning and control. Finally, good ideas with universal appeal can be used as widely as possible [4].

- Two views exist regarding the standardization of international marketing. At one extreme is the view that one basic advertising theme is desirable because one theme promotes a consistent and universally recognized company image among people of different heritages. Campbell's soup, Revlon, Union Carbide and Coca-Cola are just four of the companies that have capitalized on this idea. The opposite view is that more than one theme is desirable to respond most effectively to the cultural differences that exist among varying locales [3].

- Madison Avenue and its clients are trying to come to terms with the issue of global versus multinational advertising. In the global purists' camp the banners read, "One Sight, One Sound, One Sell," and the talk is of the cultural common denominators that will allow ads to travel well worldwide. Meanwhile, the faithful in the multinational camp hold that the marketing campaigns tailored to individual cultures are more effective and will more than pay for the additional creative and production costs [21].

Just as in the domestic market, the global marketeer must consider the "Four P's" of marketing: product, price, promotion, and placement. *Product policy* is based upon either a global, standardized, "we sell what we make" philosophy or a multinational, differentiated, "we make what we sell" philosophy. Fundamental approaches to *pricing* include full-cost pricing, incremental-cost pricing and profit-contribution pricing. *Promotion policy* can be local, international, multinational, or global depending upon the emphasis on the home market. *Placement policy* emphasizes direct distribution through the company's sales offices and personal salespersons or indirect distribution through external agencies [16, 5, 20, 8, 6].

Whatever approach a company takes to the "Four P's," it should avoid becoming the "global village idiot." There have been some incredible blunders in international marketing that could have been prevented by adequate market research. General Motors tried to market the Nova automobile in Puerto Rico; however, *no va* means "it does not go" in Spanish and there wasn't a big market in Puerto Rico for a car that does not go. In West Germany the Pepsi Cola advertising slogan, "Come alive with Pepsi," was translated as, "Come out of the grave with Pepsi." Obviously, when such large errors can occur through simple mistranslation, it doesn't take much of a marketing imagination to realize the drastic repercussions of introducing unwanted products or violating local laws. Unfortunately, mistakes are hard to avoid because the world is changing so rapidly [19].

Perhaps the biggest change in the global marketplace of the future will be a de-emphasis on the United States as the primary target market. International agreements involving economic cooperation and integration produce common markets that become the center of future global strategies. The European Economic Community (EEC), composed of Belgium, Denmark, France, Greece, Holland, Italy, Ireland, Luxembourg, Portugal, Spain, the United Kingdom and Germany, consolidates on December 31, 1992. The EEC's population of over 320 million consumers in combination with the free movement of money, goods, people, and services within the community poses a substantial threat to American dominance as the premier marketplace [18].

The United States may counter the EEC's consolidation by establishing a North American Common Market (NACM) composed of

Canada, Mexico, and the United States. While Mexico is wary of closer commercial links to the United States, a free flow of labor might provide millions of Mexican workers with employment in the United States and Canada. In turn, a growing Mexican economy would prove to be a bonanza for American business.

Even if the EEC and NACM are successful, future global strategies may center around large individual national markets such as the People's Republic of China (PRC), India, and the Soviet Union. Alternatively, potential confederations of smaller markets, like the "Four Little Tigers" (South Korea, Singapore, Hong Kong, and Taiwan), provide great opportunities for global firms. Perhaps the greatest potential market would be an economic confederation between the PRC and Hong Kong, who merge in 1997, and the remaining Three Little Tigers.

The Global Factory

In the 1980s, many international and multinational corporations were required to rationalize production to survive. "Rationalization" involves producing and assembling different product components in different parts of the world to take advantage of varying costs of labor, capital, and raw materials. For example, a global corporation might choose to manufacture complex, high-tech components in a capital rich country like Japan where it can take advantage of computer-aided manufacturing and robotics. Then the components can be shipped for assembly in a labor rich country like Mexico that is close to a large market in the United States. The result is an overall reduction in costs for the global corporation [5].

Rationalization of production created the Global Factory. By looking at the entire world as its factory, the global corporation organizes production to cut costs and increase price competitiveness. Once a global corporation gains an edge through lower costs, it can use differential pricing to cut prices in those markets where competitors need sufficient cash flow to go global. For example, if a global corporation believes that a competitor is gaining enough capital to become a threat, it can attack the competitor by providing low-priced substitute products in the competitor's home market. The competitor will have to use its excess cash to preserve its position in its home market and will not be able to globalize. Of course, the competitor may counter-attack the global firm by filing antitrust or anti-dumping complaints.

The global corporation recognizes that it may be attacked for violating antitrust laws, but is willing to take the political and legal risks. At this time, there are no enforceable international antitrust laws and none are expected. Antitrust laws are largely an American provincialism that rejects the reality of international competition and the globalization of markets. Present antitrust laws hurt American competitors who follow a code that foreign competitors can ignore [1, 25].

New global business relationships are overpowering the antitrust doctrine. Rapid technological advancement has created organizational configurations that do not fall within traditional definitions of corporations. The global factory has forced corporations to join networks of subsidiaries or teams of strategic alliances that are often "vertically disaggregated," relying on other companies for crucial business functions such as manufacturing. The new structures make it impossible to determine whether an effective monopoly exists [25].

An unsuccessful lawsuit by the United States government charging International Business Machines with monopolization of the markets illustrates the weakening of the antitrust doctrine. The unarticulated premise underlying the dismissal of the lawsuit was that antitrust law is not the proper vehicle to resolve issues raised by the globalization of industry. As the tide of antitrust cases ebb, the wave of the future will be strategic alliances such as the Toyota/ General Motors joint venture in Fremont, California [1, 28].

Summary

Futurologists forecast a continuing globalization of the world economy. Businesspeople can begin to explore globalization by scanning the world for opportunities. The corporation can actively search for opportunities or it can passively gather information in an informal manner. Many businesspeople find opportunities in a casual encounter, such as a golf game. If a corporation does not have its own intelligence department, it should gather information from government agencies, banks, or private information boutiques.

The Global Money Market provides an opportunity for corporations to take advantage of differences in tax rates, interest rates, and exchange rates to achieve significant savings. A corporation can raise capital by listing its stock in the international securities market or by tapping foreign investors for debt financing.

A de-emphasis on the United States as the primary target market necessitates entry into the Global Marketplace. Generally, firms can approach the Global Marketplace with either a global, standardized approach or a multinational, localized approach. The proper approach depends upon the match between the firm's resources and its target markets.

The Global Factory provides an opportunity for corporations to take advantage of varying costs of labor, capital, and raw materials. By rationalizing production, the corporation can lower costs and increase price competitiveness. Competitors may fight back by filing antitrust complaints; however, antitrust law isn't the proper vehicle to resolve the issues raised by globalization.

References and Suggested Readings

1. Austin, Arthur. "Antitrust Reaction to the Merger Wave: The Revolution vs. the Counterrevolution." *North Carolina Law Review.* Vol. 66, June 1988, pp. 931+.
2. Beauvois, John. "International Intelligence for the International Enterprise." *California Management Review*, Winter 1961, pp. 39–46.
3. Britt, Steuart H. "Standardizing Marketing for the International Market." *Columbia Journal of World Business*, Winter 1974, pp. 39–45.
4. Buzzell, Robert D. "Can You Standardize Multinational Marketing?" *Harvard Business Review*, November–December 1968, pp. 102–113.
5. Daniels, John D., E.W. Ogram, Jr., and L.H. Radebaugh. *International Business.* Reading, Massachusetts: Addison-Wesley Publishing Company, 1982.
6. Dymsza, William A. *Multinational Business Strategy.* New York: McGraw-Hill Book Company, 1972.
7. Eldridge, F.R. *Export and Import Practice.* Washington, D.C.: U.S. Department of Commerce, 1938.

8. "Global Marketing: Can It Work?" *Marketing & Media Decisions*, December 1984. The entire issue.
9. Keegan, Warren. "Acquisition of Global Business Information." *Columbia Journal of World Business*, March–April 1968, pp. 35–41.
10. Kent, Sherman. *Strategic Intelligence for American World Policy*. Princeton, NJ: Princeton University, 1949.
11. Kobrin, Stephen. "Strategic Integration in Fragmented Environments: Social and Political Assessment by Subsidiaries." Paper presented at Symposium on Global Competition, *Institute of International Business*. Stockholm, 1984.
12. Laqueur, Walter. *A World of Secrets: The Uses and Limits of Intelligence*. New York: Basic Books, 1985.
13. Naisbitt, John and Patricia Aburdene. *Megatrends 2000: Ten New Directions for the 1990's*. New York: William Morrow and Company, Inc., 1990.
14. Naisbitt, John. *Megatrends: Ten New Directions Transforming Our Lives*. New York: Warner Books, 1982.
15. Peters, Tom. "Closed Minds Can't Open Markets." *U.S. News & World Reports*, March 3, 1986, p. 59.
16. Rachman, D. and M. Mescon. *Business Today*. New York: Random House, 1982.
17. Radler, Albert J. "Taxation Policy in Multinational Companies." *Management International Review*, Vol. 9. No. 4–5, 1969.
18. Revzin, Philip. "United We Stand. . ." *Wall Street Journal World Business Supplement*, September 22, 1989, pp. R5–R6.
19. Ricks, David A. and Vijay Mahajan. "Blunders in International Marketing: Fact or Fiction." *Long Range Planning*, 1984, Vol. 17. No. 1, pp. 78–82.
20. Root, Franklin R. *Foreign Market Entry Strategies*. New York: AMACOM, 1982.
21. Rutigliano. Anthony J. "Global vs. Local Advertising." *Management Review*, June 1986, pp. 27–31.
22. Scherer, Ron. "Information Boutiques—Intelligence for a Price." *US News & World Report*, May 20, 1985, pp. 72–73.
23. Schwendiman, John S. *Strategic and Long-Range Planning for the Multinational Corporation*. New York: Praeger, 1973.
24. Skigen, Patricia. *Globalization of Banking: Foreign Banking in the United States*. Practicing Law Institute, 1989.

25. Thurow, Lester C. *The Zero-Sum Society.* New York: Basic Books, 1980.
26. Toffler, Alvin. *The Third Wave.* New York: William Morrow and Company, Inc., 1980.
27. ———. *Future Shock.* New York: Random House, 1970.
28. Weiss, Stephen E. "Creating the GM-Toyota Joint Venture: A Case in Complex Negotiation." *Columbia Journal of World Business*, Summer 1987, pp. 23+.
29. Yates, Ronald, R. Moseley and P. Widder. "Worldwide Trading." *The Chicago Tribune Magazine*, May 1, 1988, pp. 10+.

4
....

UNDERSTANDING CULTURE

Culture as a Problem-Solving Tool

Culture is a group problem-solving tool that enables individuals to survive in a particular environment.

Culture can be defined as:

- Traditional problem solving through accepted responses that have met with success. It consists of learned problem-solutions [5].
- Habitual and traditional ways of thinking, feeling, and reacting that are characteristic of the ways a particular society meets its problems at a particular point in time [14].

Environmental adaptation requires a "cultural map" that helps an individual interact with the group. This cultural map can be likened

43

to a relief map. Just as a person finds his way through a terrain by studying the details of a relief map, so too, a group member must memorize details and follow certain paths to effectively interact with the group.

Just as a relief map isn't the actual territory but an abstract representation of a particular area, a cultural map is an abstract description of successful problem-solving tools. Readers should be able to negotiate through society if they correctly read the map. However, cultural maps can be interpreted in many different ways. Learning to read them requires interacting over time with a particular group.

The Acquisition of Culture

With the exception of legendary wild infants, such as Romulus and Remus, who were raised by a wolf, and Tarzan, who was raised by apes, all human beings from the moment of birth enter a process called "enculturation." Through this process children become effective members of society. They observe other members relating to each other and learn guidelines for acceptable behavior. Social life would be impossible without these shared understandings and practices [1].

"Cultural traits" are unique aspects of individual cultures. A cultural trait may be a custom, such as the practice of males opening doors for females; a technological implement, such as a bow and arrow or a nuclear weapon; a gesture, such as a handshake; or an idea, such as existentialism. Certain cultural traits exist in different forms in all known cultures. (See Murdock's Universal Aspects of Culture.) Murdock's list of common cultural traits shows that even the most primitive of cultures is extremely complex [16].

"Folkways" are cultural traits that fall under the subheading of customs or habits. A person who violates the group's folkways is punished in an informal way, such as avoidance by other members or exclusion from their activities. If the group comes to believe that a folkway is necessary, it becomes part of the moral code or "mores" of the society. If the folkway must be strictly followed, then it may become part of the written laws of the society.

Murdock's Universal Aspects of Culture

Age-grading	Inheritance Rules
Athletic Sports	Joking
Bodily Adornment	Kin-groups
Calender Law	Kinship Nomenclature
Cleanliness Training	Language
Cooking	Law
Cooperative Labor	Luck Superstitions
Cosmology	Marriage
Courtship	Mealtimes
Dancing	Medicine
Decorative Art	Modesty Concerning Natural Functions
Divination	Mourning
Division of Labor	Music
Dream Interpretation	Mythology
Education	Numerals
Eschatology	Obstetrics
Ethics	Penal Sanctions
Ethnobotany	Personal Names
Etiquette	Population Policy
Faith Healing	Postnatal Care
Family	Pregnancy Usages
Feasting	Property Rights
Firemaking	Propitiation of Supernatural Beings
Folklore	Puberty Customs
Food Taboos	Religious Ritual
Funeral Rites	Residence Rules
Games	Sexual Restrictions
Gestures	Soul Concepts
Gift Giving	Status Differentiation
Government	Surgery
Greetings	Tool Making
Hair Styles	Trade
Hospitality	Visiting
Housing	Weaning
Hygiene	Weather Control
Incest Taboos	

A group of related cultural traits may become a "culture pattern" or "culture complex." Culture patterns can be as simple as a style of dress or as complex as an economic, political, or social system. An example of a simple culture pattern is the related customs of dating, courtship, and marriage.

Although enculturation within one's own society is the primary method of acquiring cultural traits, culture is acquired in other ways. Individuals often acquire cultural traits through contact with a different cultural group. Contacts can occur through neighborhood, commerce, or marriage. Each society borrows cultural traits from the other, particularly if a newly learned trait seems better than a traditional one. As a result, cultural traits spread from their origins in a process called "diffusion."

Diffusion is the most common cause of cultural change. New scientific discoveries, innovative forms of technology, and current media events cause some sectors of society to change quite rapidly. Other sectors, wary of new ideas and lifestyles, resist the changes. As new technology becomes accepted in everyday living, previously wary sectors must struggle to catch up. This phenomenon is known as "cultural lag" [18].

If contact between societies is prolonged, "acculturation" may occur. Traits that have been borrowed over the short term become permanently adopted. New customs, devices, gestures, and ideas irrevocably change both cultures [3].

"Assimilation" occurs when immigrants or other newcomers adopt the culture of the society in which they have settled. This cultural borrowing is often one-sided. The assimilated minority group eventually loses the cultural characteristics that had set it apart.

When people first leave their own culture to enter another, they must grapple with unfamiliar and unpredictable events, relationships, and objects. This often results in a phenomenon called "culture shock." In *Future Shock* (1970), Alvin Toffler describes how culture shock begins:

> Culture shock is what happens when a person suddenly finds himself
> in a place where yes may mean no, where a fixed price is negotiable,
> where to be kept waiting in an outer office is no cause for insult,

where laughter may signify anger. It is what happens when the familiar psychological clues that help an individual to function in society are suddenly withdrawn and replaced by new ones that are strange or incomprehensible.

The effects of culture shock vary from individual to individual. It is common for people to suffer from anxiety, confusion, and apathy when they are first immersed in an unfamiliar environment. The emotional stress of the situation can easily lead to emotional and intellectual withdrawal. Some people withdraw like shell-shocked soldiers or disaster victims. Other people become aggressive. The aggression can lead to increased productivity or to open warfare upon the unfamiliar ways of life [3].

Cultural Attitudes

Historically, human beings categorized human differences. Aristotle divided the world's population into Greeks and barbarians, or freemen and slaves. Classical accounts of foreign cultures emphasized strange, shocking, and degrading qualities of people under observation. This emphasis on the gulf between "we" and "they" continued into the early history of scientific observation. For example, Darwin described the Tierra del Fuegians as "wild animals."

People need a "we" identity to navigate successfully within their own culture. However, this "we" attitude creates a rift between differing cultures. In an attempt to establish superiority by proving other cultures inferior, most societies resort to ethnic name-calling attributing vices and shortcomings to the "inferior" society.

William Graham Sumner coined the term "ethnocentrism" to describe viewing one's own group as the center of everything. Each group encourages self-pride by boasting of its superiority. Group members exaggerate everything in their own folkways that sets them apart. They think their own folkways are the only right ones and look with contempt on outsiders. If a group sees other people using different folkways, it scorns them with opprobrious ephithets [15]. (See LeVine and Campbell's Ethnocentrism Framework.)

Levine & Campbell's Ethnocentrism Framework	
Attitudes and Behaviors Toward Ingroup	**Attitudes and Behaviors Toward Outgroup**
1.1 See selves as virtuous and superior	1.2 See outgroup as contemptible immoral and inferior
1.3 See own standards of value as universal, intrinsically true. See own customs as original, centrally human.	
1.4 See selves as strong	1.5 See outgroups as weak
	1.6 Social distance
	1.7 Outgroup hate
1.8 Sanctions against ingroup theft	1.9 Sanctions for outgroup theft or absence of sanctions against
1.10 Sanctions against ingroup murder	1.11 Sanctions for outgroup murder or absence of sanctions against outgroup murder
1.12 Cooperative relations with ingroups members	1.13 Absence of cooperation with outgroup members
1.14 Obedience to ingroup authorities	1.15 Absence of obedience to outgroup authorities
1.16 Willingness to remain an ingroup member	1.17 Absence of conversion to outgroup membership
1.18 Willingness to fight and die for ingroup	1.19 Absence of willingness to fight and die for outgroups
	1.20 Virtue in killing outgroup members in warfare
	1.21 Use of outgroups as bad examples in the training of children
	1.22 Blaming of outgroup for ingroup troubles
	1.23 Distrust and fear of the outgroup

Ethnocentrism is related to the more general and naive "phenomenal absolutism." Phenomenal absolutism is the tendency to assume that the world is exactly as one sees it, and that all other persons, groups or cultures perceive the world in the same way, but behave differently out of a perverse wickedness or incompetence [15].

Ethnocentrism manifests itself as "xenophobia," which is a strong dislike or distrust of foreigners. Xenophobic attitudes are inward-oriented and can lead to isolationism. By using the "ostrich defense," xenophobic societies avoid contact with differing cultures and keep themselves from being infected by foreign culture.

When a highly sophisticated culture bombards a more primitive culture with ethnocentric bias, xenophilia results. Xenophiles accept the "inherent superiority" of foreign cultures and relegate themselves to a supplicant position. In accepting their inferiority, xenophiles often adopt the superior foreign culture as their own.

"Polycentrism" is an outward-oriented form of xenophobia. Polycentric individuals interact with foreigners, normally for commercial reasons, but believe their cultures are incomprehensible and overwhelming. All cross-cultural interaction is extremely cautious because the danger of misinterpretation and conflict is high. When interaction does occur, the polycentric individual follows St. Ambrose's maxim: *Si fueris Romae, Romano vivito more; Si fueris alibi, vivito sicut ibi.*" ("When you are in Rome live in the Roman style; when you are elsewhere live as they live elsewhere.")

"Cultural relativism" is the opposite of ethnocentrism. Cultural relativists reject the ethnocentric mode of judging other cultures and deny the validity of any standard for evaluating cultural phenomena. Relativists believe that a culture can only be appropriately assessed in terms of its geographical, historical, and social context.

William Graham Sumner used the relativist doctrine to shock his contemporaries. Sumner asserted that even practices like infanticide, slavery, cannibalism, human sacrifice, and religious prostitution are comprehensible in the light of their settings as adaptations to particular sets of circumstances. As such, they must be accepted as justified, as right in an objective or scientific sense, and even, from the standpoint of their practitioners, as moral [16].

In *Patterns of Culture* (1934), Ruth Benedict further expounds upon Sumner's concept. Benedict writes that cultures must be viewed in context. Every culture is a unique configuration and can only be understood in its totality. Melville Herskovits followed this idea up in *Cultural Relativism* (1972) writing that all cultures must be accorded equal dignity and validity.

Cultural relativity is closely related to "empathy." Empathy is the generalized ability to see the world through the eyes of others. Empathetic people understand the feelings of others, place themselves in the position of others, and sense other people's reactions [3].

"Cultural empathy" is the ability to see the world as members of another culture see it. Without cultural empathy, the views and actions of members of another culture seem odd or even immoral. However, when these actions are examined from the other person's perspective, the reasons and assumptions behind the actions become clear.

Both cultural relativity and cultural empathy have been challenged. "Cultural comparativists" isolate an item, institution, process or complex from its larger cultural matrix and compare it with items, institutions, processes, or complexes in other sociocultural contexts. In *Culture and Society* (1965), George Murdock derides Herskovits' call for "equal dignity for all cultures" as sentimental nonsense. Murdock chides:

> It is one thing to respect the organization, integration, complexity, and adaptiveness of cultural systems, but quite another to insist that all are equally admirable or even equally adaptive.

Cultural empathy has been under fire as extremely difficult if not impossible. In *The Silent Language* (1973), Edward T. Hall writes:

> Culture hides much more than it reveals, and strangely enough what it hides, it hides most effectively from its own participants. Years of study have convinced me that the real job is not to understand foreign culture but to understand our own. I am also convinced that all that one ever gets from studying foreign culture is a token understanding. The ultimate reason for such study is to learn more about how one's own system works.

An over-emphasis on empathy also has been seen as undesirable. Critics suggest that people working overseas should hang onto their national characteristics and resist being incorporated into a "universal culture" [8].

Despite opposition, some proponents call for a "universal attitude" if not a universal culture. This non-national or international viewpoint is called "geocentrism." Geocentrism attempts to maximize effectiveness in intercultural relations. Superiority is not equated with nationality. The efficiency and effectiveness of cultural traits are what counts, not their origin. Geocentrism transcends cultural lines and establishes a "world orientation" [19].

Some scholars considered creating a world orientation through the development of a universal language. In the nineteenth century, Johann Martin Schleyer developed "Volapük," which was based on English and the Romance languages. Volapük thrived until Ludwik Lejzer Zamenhof, also known as Doktoro Esperanto, developed "Esperanto" in the hopes of promoting international tolerance. While Esperanto speakers can still be found today, its use has met with only limited success [2].

English may be the world's first truly universal language. While it is the native language of only 400 million people in 12 nations, another 400 million speak it as a second language. If the several hundred million people with some knowledge of English are added to the count, the number of English speakers exceeds one billion. Furthermore, hundreds of millions of people are presently studying English as a second language, including over 250 million Chinese. Considering these numbers, it should be no surprise that English is the language of international business [17].

National Character

"National character" is a system of attitudes, values, and beliefs that become dominant in a nation through common experience. For example, childrearing may follow a basic pattern, such as that presented by Dr. Benjamin Spock in *Baby and Child Care* (1946). National educational standards and methods of teaching may exist. National laws may require specified job performance. National television shows, radio programs, and magazine and newspaper articles may present similar ideas and values. Cumulatively, a wide range of similar national stimuli may cause citizens to develop similar socio-psychological characteristics [9].

Implicit in the definition of national character are four assumptions: (1) all people belonging to a certain nation are alike in some respects; (2) by the same token, they are different from other nations in the same respects; (3) the characteristics ascribed to them are in some way related to the fact that they are citizens of a given nation; and (4) the characteristics may be described in common language [4].

"Culture" can be easily confused with "national character"; however, the concepts are distinguishable in two main ways. First, a particular culture is not likely to be delineated by national boundaries because shifting borders can separate cultural groups. Second, while culture emphasizes heritage, a cumulative quality is not essential to national character because a nation can literally spring up overnight [22].

Opponents attack many early attempts to establish specific instances of national character as being too broad. They associate the generalizations that came out of national character studies with race theory and regard them as unscientific stereotypes. Furthermore, attempts at studying national character required transcending disciplinary boundaries and threatened established disciplinary viewpoints and identities [9].

National character studies involve a blending of theories from anthropology, sociology, and psychology. Some scholars harbor unjustifiable fears that these social sciences will be damaged by interdisciplinary studies.

On the other hand, the danger of racism is real and must be carefully considered. A "race" is a subdivision of mankind distinguished by common characteristics, usually physical in nature that are determined by genetic and hereditary factors. "Racism" is a belief in the inherent superiority of certain racial and ethnic groups over others, along with the corollary that the "superior" group has the right to conquer, exploit, and even destroy those considered inferior.

The idea of race, racial identity, and alleged inborn racial differences in mental capacity play a tremendous role in shaping relations between nations. Racism is used to unify nations by identifying other races as "the enemy." Racial identity can provide a strong sense of ego-enhancement and can be used to convince people that their race is unconquerable. Supposed racial defects in mental capacity have been used to justify economic exploitation and slave labor [12].

Historically, racism has been used as a rationalization for national conquest and expansion. The English attempted to make imperialism a noble activity by expounding the philosophy of the "white man's burden." Under this racist view, the white man was "destined" to bring civilization to the benighted members of other "lesser" races. The French justified maintenance of a colonial empire through their philosophy of *mission civilisatrice*, which emphasized the duty of the French people to bring civilization to the "backward" people of the world.

"Stereotypes" arise from racist viewpoints. Stereotypes are unscientific generalizations based on hearsay, anecdotes, and partial or incomplete experience, rather than on carefully collected data. National stereotypes are based upon prejudices, rather than actual observation.

To avoid reaffirming preconceived prejudices, national character studies should ensure validity. If a study involves a representative sample of members of a cultural group and analyzes adequate evidence to show that each group member has certain characteristics, then the study will arrive at inductive generalizations and not stereotypes.

To avoid the dangers of racism and prejudice, some researchers apply the statistical concept of "mode" to studies of national character. A mode is the most frequent value in a frequency distribution. When two values are *about equal* in maximum frequency, the distribution is described as "bimodal." Distributions with several modes are "multimodal" [11]. (See Table 4-1.)

By changing their focus from national character to "modal personality structure," researchers take into account the possibility that a great variety of individual personality characteristics and patternings exists in any society. A modal personality structure is one which appears with considerable frequency in a population; several modal personality structures may exist in any population [9 and 4].

A multimodal conception of national character seems to be the most meaningful as well as the most empirically realistic. It is unlikely that any specific personality characteristic, or character type, will be found in as much as 60 or 70 percent of any modern national

Table 4-1
The Concept of Mode

Example # 1: Determine the mode for the number of cars sold.
Eight salespeople sell the following number of cars:

Salesperson # 1: 5 cars	Salesperson # 5: 14 cars
Salesperson # 2: 11 cars	Salesperson # 6: 23 cars
Salesperson # 3: 6 cars	Salesperson # 7: 11 cars
Salesperson # 4: 11 cars	Salesperson # 8: 3 cars

More salespeople sold 11 cars then any other number of cars. The mode in this example is the value with the greatest frequency. Mode = 11

Example # 2: Determine the mode for the number of cars sold.
Eight salespeople sell the following number of cars:

Salesperson # 1: 9 cars	Salesperson # 5: 11 cars
Salesperson # 2: 11 cars	Salesperson # 6: 23 cars
Salesperson # 3: 9 cars	Salesperson # 7: 11 cars
Salesperson # 4: 11 cars	Salesperson # 8: 9 cars

Four salespeople sold 11 cars and three sold 9 cars. This distribution is "bimodal." Mode = 11 and 9

Example # 3: Determine the mode for the number of cars sold.
Eight salespeople sell the following number of cars:

Salesperson # 1: 10 cars	Salesperson # 5: 9 cars
Salesperson # 2: 11 cars	Salesperson # 6: 10 cars
Salesperson # 3: 10 cars	Salesperson # 7: 11 cars
Salesperson # 4: 11 cars	Salesperson # 8: 9 cars

Three salespeople sold 11 cars, three sold 10 cars, and two sold 9 cars. This distribution is "multimodal." Mode = 10; 11; 9

population. However, it is reasonable to assume that a nation may be characterized by a limited number of modes. A single nation may contain five or six modes which apply anywhere from 10 to 30 percent of the total population. Such a conception of national character accommodates subcultural variations, such as socioeconomic status, religion, and degree of urbanization, that exist in all modern nations [9].

Studies of modal personality structure can distinguish the sociopsychological characteristics of specific segments of a nation, such as professionals. As businesspersons, doctors, and lawyers move up the professional ladder, they are often socialized to a common way of thinking. The socialization process perpetuates similar beliefs, attitudes, and values among successive policy-making groups. Professionals who do not assimilate may be ostracized or even expelled from the professional organization.

For example, the socialization of prospective American attorneys is designed to make them "think like lawyers." Prospective entrants are indoctrinated with beliefs, attitudes, and values such as "there is no law" and "the law is not concerned with justice." Such attitudes are confusing to the general populace, which believes that there is law and that the law is fundamentally concerned with justice. However, a prospective attorney must assimilate the values of established professionals or risk rejection by the bar.

Determining what modal personality structures exist in a given nation is difficult. A proper study requires individual psychological investigations of an adequately large and representative sample of the populace. Financial constraints, inappropriate testing devices, linguistic difficulties, inability to obtain accurate samples, problems with data collection, inaccuracy of information, restrictions on transborder data flows, and, ultimately, problems with the generalization of findings limit such studies.

Most national character studies rely upon modified cultural anthropological approaches. Cultural anthropology infers values from collective phenomenon, from verbal statements about the predominance of values, and from generalizations made on the basis of individual behavior. It is not uncommon to see studies which rely upon an analysis of collective policies, cultural products, journal articles, research reports, and personal interviews. Such studies are largely impressionistic, rather than rigorously empirical [4].

Summary

Anthropology provides hundreds of definitions of culture. Perhaps the best way to think of culture is as a map that shows people how to get from point A to point B in a particular environment. From the moment children are born, they begin to be enculturated into common ways of solving problems. Other cultural traits are acquired from neighboring societies by diffusion. If contact with another culture is prolonged, acculturation occurs and both cultures are irrevocably changed.

When people are immersed in a foreign culture, they begin to assimilate new cultural traits. Unpredictable and unfamiliar ways of solving problems may cause culture shock. The resulting stress may lead to emotional and intellectual withdrawal. Alternatively, the visitor can have an ethnocentric reaction and attack the other culture's "inferior" methods. Xenophobes strongly dislike and distrust foreigners. Xenophiles accept their culture's "inferiority."

Polycentric people want to interact with foreigners, but lack understanding of them. The ability to see the world through the eyes of foreigners is called cultural empathy. Some scientists believe that it is impossible to achieve more than a token understanding of a foreign culture.

National character refers to attitudes, values, and beliefs that are dominant in a nation's populace. Care must be taken to avoid the use of national character studies to reinforce preconceived notions and prejudices. By emphasizing modal personality structure, researchers expressly recognize that many cultures may exist in one nation.

References and Suggested Readings

1. Benedict, Ruth. *Patterns of Culture.* New York: Mentor Books, 1934, 1953.
2. Boulton, Marjorie. *Zamenhof: Creator of Esperanto,* 1960.
3. Brislin, Richard W. *Cross-Cultural Encounters.* New York: Pergamon Press, 1981.
4. Duijker, H. and N. Frijda. *National Character and National Stereotypes.* Amsterdam: North-Holland Publishing Co., 1960.
5. Ford, C.S. "Culture and Human Behavior." *Scientific Monthly,* Vol. 55, 1942, pp. 546–547.
6. Hall, Edward T. *The Silent Language.* Garden City, New York: Anchor Press, 1973.
7. Herskovits, Melville J. *Cultural Relativism.* New York: Random House, 1972.

8. Hill, Roy. "Once a Frenchman always a Frenchman." *International Management*, June 1980, pp. 46–47.
9. Inkeles, Alex and Daniel J. Levinson. "National Character: The Study of Modal Personality and Sociocultural Systems." in G. Lindzey & E. Aronson (eds.) *The Handbook of Social Psychology*. Reading, Mass.: Addison-Wesley, 1969.
10. Jacobs, Melville. *Patterns in Cultural Anthropology*. Homewood, Illinois: Dorsey Press, 1964.
11. Kazmier, Leonard. *Business Statistics*. New York: McGraw-Hill Book Company, 1976.
12. Klineberg, Otto. *The Human Dimension in International Relations*. New York: Holt, Rinehart & Winston, 1966.
13. Kluckhohn, Clyde and A.L. Kroeber. *Culture*. New York: Vintage Books, 1963.
14. Kluckhohn, Clyde and D. Leighton. *The Navaho*. Cambridge: Harvard University Press, 1946.
15. LeVine, Robert A. and Donald T. Campbell. *Ethnocentrism*. New York: John Wiley & Sons, Inc., 1972.
16. Murdock, George P. *Culture and Society*. Pittsburgh: University of Pittsburgh Press, 1965.
17. Naisbitt, John and Patricia Aburdene. *Megatrends 2000: Ten New Directions for the 1990's*. New York: William Morrow and Company, Inc., 1990.
18. Ogburn, William F. *On Culture and Social Change: Selected Papers*. Chicago: University of Chicago Press, 1964.
19. Perlmutter, Howard V. "The Torturous Evolution of the Multinational Corporation." *Columbia Journal of World Business*, January–February 1969.
20. Spock, Dr. Benjamin. *Baby and Child Care*, 1946.
21. Sumner, William G. *Folkways*, 1906.
22. Terhune, K. "From National Character to National Behavior." *Journal of Conflict Resolution*. Vol. XIV, No. 2.
23. Toffler, Alvin. *Future Shock*. New York: Random House, 1970.
24. Tylor, Sir Edward B. *Primitive Culture*, Boston, 1871.
25. Wagner, Roy. *The Invention of Culture*. Chicago: University of Chicago Press, 1981.

5

·········

DEVELOPING A GEOCENTRIC CORPORATE CULTURE

"Mr. Podsnap"

In *Our Mutual Friend* (1865) Charles Dickens develops a character known as Mr. Podsnap. Podsnap is a well-to-do Englishman who makes his living through world trade. Ironically, he thinks that other countries are "a mistake." In discussing foreign manners and customs, Podsnap conclusively observes "Not English!" and dismisses them "with a flourish of the arm and a flush of the face." After much soul searching, Podsnap invites a foreign gentleman to a dinner party. At the party, Podsnap and the other guests treat the foreigner "as if he were a child who was hard of hearing." Engaging his foreign guest in a conversation, Podsnap continually berates him for improper pronunciation of the English language: "We do not say 'Ozer'; we say 'Other': the letters are 'T' and 'H'; you say 'Tay' and 'Aish', You Know."

In discussing politics, Podsnap expresses great pride in the English constitution: "It Was Bestowed Upon Us By Providence.

No Other Country is so Favoured as This Country." When the foreign guest asks how other countries manage, Podsnap replies with a grave shake of his head: "they do—I am sorry to be obliged to say it—*as* they do." Podsnap then expounds on the virtues of being an Englishman. After talking to his guest, Podsnap's face flushes as he thinks of the remote possibility that some "prejudiced" foreign citizens might disagree with his evaluation. So, "with his favourite right-arm flourish, he put the rest of Europe and the whole of Asia, Africa, and America nowhere."

The Failure of "Podsnappery"

Mr. Podsnap lives in a small world, both morally and geographically. He can despise the rest of the world, yet still make his fortune from it. "Podsnappery" means a disdain for cultural differences in international business transactions. In Podsnap's time, podsnappery was useful as a survival mechanism. It bound English businessmen into a cohesive unit in their quest to build the British Empire [17].

In the modern world, podsnappery is both outmoded and dysfunctional. American CEOs who are going global find that skills that were successful in the U.S. market aren't effective in foreign cultures. For example, when construction company managers from five different countries formed a strategic alliance, they found it difficult to cooperate on their Latin American project. The manager of an American engineering company in Africa was repeatedly thrown in jail when his business discussions escalated into exchanges of insults and punches [10, 7, 24, 3].

Global business executives must recognize and understand differences in business attitudes and the meaning of contracts. Trade negotiators must enter a negotiating session anywhere in the world with the confidence and ability to manage the cultural differences of the representatives. Lawyers must develop a talent for establishing legal protections without creating an atmosphere of distrust that would impede the flow of business. Businesspeople must develop a world view and a geocentric corporate culture.

Corporate Culture

Management theory is awash in buzzwords. Businesspeople can read about theories X, Y, and Z; quantitative management, portfolio management, management by objectives, management by walking around, and one-minute management; T-groups, Grid-groups, quality circles, and skunk camps; restructuring, demassing, and raiding; computerization, diversification, zero-based budgeting, and the experience curve; intrapreneuring, outsourcing, and sticking to the basics; strategy, synergy, and strategic alliances; and internationalization, multinationalization, and globalization.

The buzzwords represent good ideas. Unfortunately, many businesspeople latch on to any management idea that looks like a quick fix. One corporate chairman heard about "corporate culture" and told his president: "This corporate culture stuff is great. I want a culture by Monday". It would be nice if there were easy solutions to difficult problems, but as Thomas Edison said: "There is no substitute for hard work." Corporate culture is not an easy concept to understand, but is worth spending time on because it is extremely important [2].

Corporate culture derives from two principal sources: (1) the cultural problem-solving maps that founders, leaders, and corporate employees bring with them when they join the company, and (2) the actual experiences that people in the company have had in resolving problems, especially crises, of external adaptation and internal integration. Corporate culture arises from the interaction of old cultural maps with new learning experiences of corporate members [15].

The Concept of Corporate Culture

- Companies as well as countries have distinctive cultures [21].
- An organization's culture is multidimensional, encompassing ideas and concepts, customs and traditions, procedures and habits for coping in a particular macroculture. It is an interwoven fabric that helps people in the microculture achieve

(continued on next page)

(continued)
   objectives and preserve values. It represents an interplay of
   diverse economic, technological, educational, and political
   subsystems, as well as social, value, and belief systems [8].
- Culture implies values, such as aggressiveness, defensive-
  ness, or nimbleness, that set a pattern for a company's
  activities, opinions, and actions. Managers instill that pattern
  in employees through example and pass it down to succeed-
  ing generations of workers. The CEO's words alone do not
  produce culture; rather, his actions and those of his managers do [4].
- Organizational culture consists of a set of symbols, ceremonies, and myths that communicate the underlying values
  and beliefs of that organization to its employees [18].
- Corporate culture consists of guiding concepts and shared
  values [20].
- Values and a spirit are at the foundation of a corporation's
  organization and management. These values are the deeply
  held beliefs, often unarticulated, that are the product of the
  culture's conditioning, its heroes, myths, and fears [12].
- Corporate culture consists of an organization's norms, values, and unwritten rules of conduct, as well as its management style, priorities, beliefs, and interpersonal behaviors.
  They create a climate that influences employee communication, planning, and decision making [23].
- Management culture includes operating philosophy and principles, leadership style, organization, and management systems. The general management culture of any given country
  is a product of the ethnic culture that surrounds it [11].
- Every company has its own word or phrase to describe culture. Some of these are "style," "our way of doing things,"
  "shared attitudes, assumptions and beliefs," "purpose,"
  "philosophy," "identity," and "ethos." To most managers,
  these are almost synonymous terms [15].

Corporate culture influences most aspects of the organization,
management, and performance of a business. A manager's task is to

develop and maintain a culture that (1) promotes efficient performance of the highest quality and quantity; (2) fosters creativity; (3) stimulates enthusiasm for effort, experimentation, innovation, and change; (4) takes advantage of interaction situations; and (5) finds new challenges [1].

A firm must choose an international or global strategy that matches its cultural problem-solving map. Culture can make or break a firm's efforts to adapt to the changing world environment. If an international or global implementation strategy violates an organization's culture, it will fail. Employees have been known to resist and actually sabotage operational changes that oppose traditional ways of conducting business [4].

If a firm is planning to globalize, it must identify its corporate culture. (See Framework for Developing a Global Strategy in Chapter 2.) The analysis should identify the values and problem-solving methods of owners, managers, and employees. The cultural analyst should pay particular attention to corporate decision-making processes, organizational structure, formal procedures, reward systems, compliance with organizational requirements, regulation and control processes, the accuracy of communication, makeup and support of dominant coalitions, and responsiveness to change.

Corporations cannot afford to keep cultures that prevent global survival strategies. If the internal audit shows that corporate culture will impede global survival, then the corporation must *actively* change its culture. Change will not occur merely by sending someone to school, hiring new staff, or acquiring new businesses. Even persuasion by the CEO won't work. Change must occur by establishing new structures, role models, and rewards and punishments.

To manage change, businesspeople should follow certain broad maxims. First, recognize that managers and employees will be more willing to accept change if they are included in the decision-making process. Second, establish open communications to reinforce trust that will be shaken by the change. Third, provide training and counseling for managers and employees who don't have the required skills and abilities to carry out the new plans. Fourth, allow enough time for the change to take hold. Fifth, emphasize that the purpose of the change is to implement a new strategic vision [5].

Corporations need strong cultures to meet global challenges. Organizations of the future may be "atomized." They will be a coalition of small, task-focused work units linked through advanced telecommunications and bound into a "corporate molecule" by shared cultural ties. Strong corporate cultures will bring a quasi-religious tone to their operations by creating heroes for managers and employees to emulate [5].

Corporate Culture and Globalization

Corporate culture is an important part of a company's global competitiveness. Differences in cultural problem-solving methods can either help or inhibit a firm's ability to conduct effective global operations. If the cultural traits of subsidiaries or allies are dysfunctional, the corporation can encourage the assimilation of its corporate problem-solving methods.

Corporate culture and strategy must mesh closely. Different environments require different strategies and different corporate cultures. Strategies for world trade and investment can be international, multinational, regional, or global. (See Chapter 2.) A cultural philosophy controls each of these strategies.

Companies involved in world trade and investment have four cultural philosophies: ethnocentrism, polycentrism, regiocentrism, and geocentrism. Each philosophy is linked to an organizational type and a strategic process. For example, the internationalization process can be linked to an ethnocentric organization [9]. (See Table 5-1.)

Table 5-1
The Relationship Between
Cultural Perspective and Strategic Choice

Cultural Perspective	Type of Company	Strategic Process
Ethnocentric	International	Internationalization
Polycentric	Multinational	Multinationalization
	Transnational or	
Regiocentric	Multiregional	Transnationalization
Geocentric	Global	Globalization

Ethnocentric Organizations

These are home-country oriented organizations. For example, when a Japanese corporation invests in Mexico, Japan is the home country and Mexico is the host country. If the Japanese corporation is ethnocentric, it will expect Mexicans to be xenophilic and accept the inherent superiority of Japan. Investments will be made on condition that Mexico accept Japanese methods of conducting business. The ethnocentric message is: "This works in Japan; therefore, it must work in Mexico."

Ethnocentric corporations believe that home-country nationals are more intelligent, reliable, and trustworthy than foreign nationals. They center all key management positions at the domestic headquarters and recruit home-country nationals for all international positions. Foreign managers and employees are second-class corporate citizens. When rewards are distributed, home-country nationals receive the lion's share.

Many internal and external influences foster this approach. Owner and stockholder perceptions may limit the CEO's power. Labor unions may impose intense pressure in favor of domestic employment. Home-government policy may force emphasis on the domestic market.

Many international companies exhibit this ethnocentric philosophy. The standard international company has difficulty communicating in different languages and accepting cultural differences. It limits international strategic alternatives to entry modes such as exporting, licensing, and turnkey operations because "it works at home and will work overseas" [19].

Polycentric Organizations

These organizations are host-country oriented. They see profit potential in a foreign country, but find the foreign market difficult to understand. The polycentric firm establishes multinational operations on condition that host-country managers "do it their way." The polycentric message is: "Local people know what is best for them. Let's give them some money and leave them alone as long as they make us a profit."

The polycentric firm is a loosely connected group with quasi-independent subsidiaries as profit centers. Home-country nationals staff headquarters, while local nationals occupy key positions in their respective local subsidiaries. No foreign national can seriously aspire to a senior position at headquarters. Host-country nationals have high or absolute sovereignty over the subsidiary's operations. There is no direction from headquarters and the only controls are financially oriented [19].

Great external pressures often necessitate a firm's adopting a polycentric approach. Foreign laws may require managers to be citizens of the host country. Engineering standards may have to be determined locally. The host-country government may be a major customer and insist upon local ways of doing business.

Many multinational corporations adopt the polycentric philosophy. The standard multinational corporation faces a heterogeneous environment in which product needs and preferences are diverse and governmental restrictions may be severe. Strategically, the multinational competes on a market-by-market basis because "local people know what is best for them."

Regiocentric Organization

These are regionally oriented organizations. A corporation implements a regional strategy when synergistic benefits can be gained by sharing common functions across regions. The corporation believes that only regional insiders can effectively coordinate functions within the region. For example, a regiocentric organization might select a Japanese subsidiary to manage its Asian operations and a French subsidiary to manage its European operations. The regiocentric message is: "Regional insiders know what neighboring countries want."

The regiocentric firm is highly interdependent on a regional basis. Regional headquarters organize collaborative efforts among local subsidiaries. The regional headquarters is responsible for the regional plan, local research and development, product innovation, cash management, local executive selection and training, capital expenditure plans, brand policy, and public relations. The world headquarters manages world strategy, country analysis, basic research and development, foreign exchange, transfer pricing, intercompany loans, long-term financing, selection of top management, technology transfer, and establishing corporate culture [16].

The regiocentric approach may become more common as various economic communities evolve. The solidification of the EEC in 1992 may spur the development of a North American Common Market and even an Asian Common Market (Japan, People's Republic of China, South Korea, Taiwan, and Singapore). With such a scenario, a regiocentric approach would be extremely functional.

Geocentric Organization

These organizations are world-oriented. The ultimate goal is creation of an integrated system with a worldwide approach. The geocentric system is highly interdependent. Subsidiaries are no longer satellites and independent city-states. The entire organization focuses on worldwide and local objectives. Every part of the organization makes a unique contribution using its unique competencies. The geocentric message is: "All for one and one for all. We will work together to solve problems anywhere in the world."

Geocentrism requires collaboration between headquarters and subsidiaries to establish universal standards with permissible local variations. Geocentric organizations integrate diverse regions through global decision making, making possible a flow of ideas between countries. They allocate resources on a global basis, erase geographical lines, and globalize functional and product lines.

Within legal and political limits, the corporation seeks the best people to solve problems. Competence is what counts, not national origin. The reward system motivates managers to surrender national biases and work for worldwide objectives.

The geocentric firm overcomes political barriers by turning its subsidiaries into good citizens of the host nations. It hopes the subsidiary will become a leading exporter from the host to the international community. Furthermore, the geocentric organization provides base countries with an increasing supply of hard currency, new skills, and a knowledge of advanced technology [19].

Going Geocentric

For geocentrism to work, corporate culture must override national cultural differences. This is not an easy task. People are reluctant to learn new problem-solving skills when they already have effective cultural maps for their local environments. Inexperience, mutual distrust, nationalistic tendencies, and immobility of top managers impede development of a geocentric perspective.

Geocentrism requires total commitment by owners, managers, and employees. The greatest responsibility falls on the shoulders of the CEO who must visit as many markets and subsidiaries as possible. He cannot go on whirlwind tours, but must conduct detailed meetings with middle managers, customers, and government officials. This globetrotting often involves a brutal schedule that can take a heavy toll on family life and personal health.

One of the CEO's primary tasks on the road is to encourage management teams to meet the challenges of globalization and assure them that they will be rewarded for doing so. The subsidiaries must make sure that the information given to the CEO does not reflect national bias. For globalization to work, the CEO must be knowledgeable of critical world events and continually monitor subsidiary understanding of social, political, and economic objectives in the host countries.

One way to encourage middle managers to adopt a geocentric perspective is to use transition rituals. Within this process, people mourn the passage of old ways and renegotiate new values and relationships. This can help middle managers understand, accept, and believe in the geocentric philosophy.

Problems in Going Geocentric

Problems may arise in creating a geocentric corporate culture. National culture and traditional corporate culture may clash with the assumptions underlying geocentrism. Some forecasters see a backlash of cultural nationalism. In the face of growing globalization and homogenization, countries and cultures may try to strictly preserve their religious, cultural, linguistic, national, and racial identities [13].

Some scholars are frightened by geocentrism and globalization. They believe that corporations will use multiple transfers of managers and executives to encourage loss of national identity. The "global cadre" of executives will identify solely with the corporation. Even family identity will be jeopardized. Members of these "global clans" will be men and women without countries. Executives and managers will become little more than corporate mercenaries [22].

Other scholars are excited by geocentrism and globalization. They believe that senior executives who build geocentric enterprises will be the most important social architects of the 1990s. In their view, geocentrism and globalization promise a greater sharing of wealth and consequent control of divisive centrifugal forces in the global community. The geocentric enterprise will make war less likely because attacking customers, suppliers, and employees is not in anyone's interest. In this view, world peace will come through world trade [14 and 19].

Summary

Corporate culture derives from the cultural problem-solving maps that founders, leaders and corporate employees bring with them when they join the company and from the actual experiences that people in the company have in resolving problems. Companies involved in world trade and investment have four cultural philosophies: ethnocentrism, polycentrism, regiocentrism, and geocentrism.

Ethnocentric organizations are home-country oriented. All key management positions are at the domestic headquarters. Many international companies follow an ethnocentric philosophy.

Polycentric organizations are host-country oriented. Headquarters is manned by home-country nationals, while local nationals occupy the key positions in their respective local subsidiaries. Many MNCs exhibit polycentrism.

Regiocentric organizations are regionally oriented. Regional headquarters organize collaborative efforts among local subsidiaries. The regiocentric approach may become more common as various economic communities evolve.

Geocentric organizations are world-oriented. Geocentrism requires collaboration between headquarters and subsidiaries to establish universal standards with permissible local variations. The geocentric approach is rapidly becoming a prerequisite for corporate survival.

Geocentrism requires total commitment by owners, managers, and employees. The greatest burden falls upon the CEO who often must follow a brutal schedule of meetings around the world. However, the rewards of globalization are worth the effort.

References and Suggested Readings

1. Blake, Robert R. and Jane S. Mouton. *The Managerial Grid.* Houston, Texas: Gulf Publishing Company, 1964.
2. Byrne, John A. "Business Fads: What's In—And Out." *Business Week,* January 20, 1986, pp. 52+.
3. Clutterbuck, David. "Breaking Through the Cultural Barrier." *International Management,* December 1980, pp. 41–42.
4. "Corporate Culture." *Business Week,* October 27, 1980, pp. 148+.
5. Deal, Terrence E. and Allan A. Kennedy. *Corporate Cultures.* Reading, Mass.: Addison-Wesley Publishing Co., 1982.
6. Dickens, Charles. *Our Mutual Friend.* London: Oxford University Press, 1885, 1990.
7. Hall, Edward T. "The Silent Language in Overseas Business." *Harvard Business Review,* May–June 1960, pp. 87–96.
8. Harris, Philip R. and Robert T. Moran. *Managing Cultural Differences.* Houston: Gulf Publishing Company, 1979.
9. Heenan, David A. and H.V. Perlmutter. *Multinational Organization Development: A Social Architectural Perspective.* Reading, Mass.: Addison-Wesley Publishing Co., 1979.
10. Holstein, William J. "Going Global." *Business Week,* October 20, 1989, pp. 9–18.
11. Masterson, Bob and Bob Murphy. "Internal Cross-Cultural Management." *Training and Development Journal,* April 1986, pp. 56–60.
12. Miller, Lawrence M. *American Spirit: Visions of a New Corporate Culture.* New York: William Morrow and Co., 1984.

13. Naisbitt, John and Patricia Aburdene. *Megatrends 2000*. New York: William Morrow and Company, 1990.
14. Naisbitt, John. *Megatrends*. New York: Warner Books, 1982.
15. Nixon, Bill. "You Can't Ignore Corporate Culture." *Accountancy*, May 1987, pp. 99–101.
16. Ohmae, Kenichi. *Triad Power*. New York: The Free Press, 1985.
17. Oppenheimer, Franz M. "Notes on Podsnappery." *Harvard Business Review*, July–August 1959, pp. 74–78.
18. Ouchi, William G. *Theory Z*. Redding, MA: Addison-Wesley Publishing Company, 1981.
19. Perlmutter, Howard V. "The Torturous Evolution of the Multinational Corporation." *Columbia Journal of World Business*, January–February 1969.
20. Peters, Thomas J. and Robert H. Waterman. *In Search of Excellence*. New York: Harper & Row, Inc., 1982.
21. Rassam, Clive. "When Company Culture Counts." *International management*, September 1976, pp. 22–23.
22. Schneider, Susan. "National vs. Corporate Culture: Implications for Human Resource Management." *Human Resource Management*, Summer 1988, Vol. 27, No. 2, pp. 231–246.
23. Senn, Dr. Larry. "Corporate Culture." *Management World*, April–May 1986, pp. 16–18.
24. Wippman, Lawrence. "Blending Five Cultures in One Big Project." *International Management*, September 1983, pp. 29+.

6

....

NEGOTIATION
AND CULTURE

Negotiating in Ancient Rome

It seems every book written about negotiation suggests a new definition. However, negotiation is an old concept. The ancient Romans used the word *negotiari*, meaning "to carry on business." *Negotiari* derives from the Latin root words *neg* (not) and *otium* (ease or leisure), meaning "not leisure." Obviously, for the ancient Romans, negotiation and business involved hard work.

Today, almost 2,000 years after the word first appeared in ancient Rome, scholars and consultants finally understand why the Romans defined negotiation as leisure-denying. Just reading all the definitions is hard work [11].

While the definitions of negotiation are different, the basic elements are the same. Close examination of the definitions reveal negotiation always involves: (1) two or more parties; (2) with common interests; (3) and conflicting interests; (4) who enter a process of interaction; (5) with the goal of reaching an agreement.

Negotiation is, therefore, a process in which two or more entities come together to discuss common and conflicting interests in order to reach an agreement of mutual benefit.

Negotiating with Princes

While definitions differ, certain immutable principles of negotiation haven't changed for thousands of years. Advice such as "know your counterpart," "study the foreign terrain," and "keep an adequate record" was as valuable in ancient Rome and eighteenth-century France as it is today.

Monsieur Francois de Callieres was a diplomat during the seventeenth and eighteenth centuries. As an ambassador extraordinary to the courts of Europe, Monsieur de Callieres became intimately familiar with the art of negotiation. His description of the immutable principles of negotiation has never been equalled.

On the Manner of Negotiating with Princes (1716) contains classic advice on who should be selected as a negotiator and what a good negotiator must do to succeed. According to Monsieur de Callieres, the art of negotiation is extremely important, and great care must be taken in choosing negotiators. Companies often send negotiators to foreign lands who are not familiar with the interests, laws, customs, language, or even geography of the country; however, no job is more difficult than negotiation.

Effective Negotiators

Skilled negotiators have observant minds, sound judgment, and a tranquil and patient nature. They have an appreciation for humor, but refuse to be distracted by pleasures or frivolous amusements. They are always ready to listen with attention to those whom they meet. Their manner of speaking is open, genial, civil, and agreeable. Effective negotiators have the presence of mind to find a quick reply to unforeseen surprises. They possess that mental penetration that enables them to discover how their counterparts are feeling and what they are thinking about. Above all, good negotiators must have sufficient control to resist the longing to speak before they have really thought about what to say.

Negotiators should thoroughly understand the purpose of the negotiation before going overseas. They should be knowledgeable of their CEO's philosophy and be prepared to cope with any unforeseen circumstances that may arise.

Negotiators must know the history of the countries with which they are dealing, the laws and established customs, the form of government, and the background of their counterparts. However, knowledge of foreign lands cannot be found in books alone. It is better to gather information by personal communication with those who have traveled to the lands in question.

Before going overseas, negotiators should contact former ambassadors, businesspeople, and others who have lived in the target country, "to acquire from them all the knowledge which they may possess". Negotiators should also contact the ambassador currently posted in the foreign country. Ambassadors can often provide letters of recommendation and introduce negotiators to important politicians and businesspeople [3].

Unfortunately, while negotiators should be given time to study the foreign environment and make necessary business contacts before going overseas, they are often sent on the spur of the moment. Therefore, negotiators must be able to make quick studies of the foreign country. They should become watchful, silent observers of the habits and customs of the country, corporations, and people they meet.

When negotiators arrive in a foreign country, they should use any sources of information that are available. It is possible to develop a "freemasonry" of global business negotiators through which one negotiator will inform another of threats and opportunities that are not common knowledge. Fellow businesspeople can be helpful. Competitors may provide assistance if they can be assured of reciprocity later on.

Negotiators should learn the history of the country they are visiting in order to interpret current events in the light of past history. More importantly, negotiators can improve their standing in the eyes of their foreign counterparts by showing an interest in foreign culture and history. The time spent studying will be amply repaid by the smoothness of the negotiations.

Negotiators should adapt to the ways and customs of the host country without showing repugnance or expressing contempt, remembering they cannot expect a whole nation to change its way of living. It is more reasonable, and in the long run much more comfortable, to adapt to foreign ways.

Negotiators shouldn't criticize the form of government or the personal conduct of government officials in the nation they are visiting. On the contrary, they should always praise that which is praiseworthy without affectation and without flattery. If negotiators properly understand the function of negotiation, they will quickly discover that every nation has many good points, excellent laws, and charming customs as well as bad ones. It is easy to single out the good points and there is no profit in denouncing the bad, because nothing the negotiators can say or do will alter the domestic habits or laws of the country they are visiting.

Good negotiators will never make promises that they cannot keep or negotiate in bad faith. No doubt deceit has been used with success in some negotiations; however, any concession gained dishonestly will have an uncertain result because the deceived party will have a long-standing desire for vengeance.

Negotiators should emphasize mutual benefit. Undoubtedly, the surest way for a negotiator to establish good relations with foreign negotiators is to prove that an agreement is of mutual advantage. The secret of negotiation is to point out the common advantages to both parties and to link these advantages so that they appear to be equally balanced.

Notes and Reports

Perhaps the most important task of a negotiator is to keep exact and faithful written accounts of the negotiations and of all other business that arises overseas. Detailed reports should begin with arrival in the foreign country and proceed to step-by-step accounts of everything that occurs. An adept negotiator's report will not only describe the negotiations but will present the essential background information for the negotiations.

The report should contain written portraits of everyone the negotiator deals with. If the negotiator is successful in painting the portrait, headquarters will feel as though they themselves had been abroad and participated in the negotiations.

The negotiator should give personal comments and hypothesize on the negotiation's success or failure. Facts and events should be included in chronological order so that headquarters can judge the merits of the negotiator's analysis. A report that merely recites facts, without discussing them in the light of the motives and policies of the foreign negotiators, is nothing more than an empty chronicle.

The best reports are written in a clear and concise manner. Simplicity is essential, and negotiators should take care to avoid all affectations such as pretending to be either witty or scholarly. The report doesn't have to be long, for even the fullest discussion of motive and circumstance can be presented in a concise form; the more concise and clear it is, the more headquarters will appreciate it.

Negotiators should write their reports as separate short articles, each focusing on a single special point. A shrewd negotiator once said that a report written in orderly fashion and in several short clear paragraphs was "like a palace lighted by many windows so that there was not a dark corner in it."

Negotiators should take daily notes of the principal points of their presentation. Immediately after leaving a negotiating session or business meeting, they should write down their recollection of what was said, how it was said, and how it was received.

The best method of making daily notes is through a diary, which is a valuable part of a negotiator's equipment. A diary is of assistance in writing reports and provides a means for refreshing a negotiator's memory at any later date. Of course, as secrecy is essential, negotiators may wish to write everything, including their diaries, in cipher.

While Monsieur de Callieres' advice was written for eighteenth-century royalty, it is still valuable today. Global business negotiators would be wise to purchase *On the Manner of Negotiating with Princes* for their negotiation library.

Warriors and Shopkeepers

Sir Harold Nicolson wrote that Monsieur de Callieres' book was "the best manual of diplomatic method ever written". This was quite a compliment coming from an Englishman to a Frenchman. Nicolson categorizes international negotiators into archetypes. In *Diplomacy,* he identifies two main currents of diplomatic theory: the "warrior" (German) theory and the "shopkeeper" (English) theory. Warriors regard diplomacy as war by other means. Shopkeepers regard diplomacy as an aid to peaceful commerce [15]. (See Table 6-1.)

Table 6-1
Two Main Theories
Of Diplomacy

	Warriors	Shopkeepers
Theory:	Heroic	Mercantile
Tendency:	Power Politics	Profit Politics
Concern:	National Prestige	National Wealth
Diplomacy:	War	Commerce
Aims of Diplomacy:	Predatory	Conciliatory
Negotiation:	Military Campaign	Business Transaction
Purpose of Negotiation:	Victory	Compromise
Objective:	Create Fear	Inspire Confidence
Tactics:	Deceit & Trickery	Honesty & Fair Play

From: Diplomacy NY: Oxford University Press. 1964.

Under the warrior concept, diplomacy is an unremitting activity directed towards ultimate triumph. The strategy of negotiation is to out-flank the opponent, to occupy strategical positions that are at once consolidated before any further advance is made; to weaken the enemy by all manner of attacks between the lines; to constantly seek to drive a wedge between the enemy and its allies; and to hold opponents to one position while planning an attack on another.

Under the shopkeeper concept, compromise between rivals is more profitable than destruction of the rival. Negotiation is an attempt to reach some durable understanding. "National honor" is interpreted as "national honesty." Questions of prestige are not allowed to interfere with sound business deals. Some middle point exists between the negotiators which, if discovered, will reconcile their conflicting interests. Finding the middle point requires a frank discussion, placing your cards on the table, and using human reason, confidence, and fair dealing.

How Nations Negotiate

While Nicolson divides negotiating styles into national archetypes, other scholars argue that national negotiating styles are rare. In *How Nations Negotiate*, Fred Ikle asserts that negotiating styles of Western governments are normally overshadowed by the styles of individual negotiators. Diplomats differ in training and cultural tradition; however, the differences are usually not pervasive enough to produce a distinctly recognizable negotiating style [10].

Despite his hesitancy to acknowledge national negotiating styles, Ikle cites certain commonalities: American diplomats are sensitive to public opinion; French diplomats use ornate historical-philosophical themes as a background to their negotiating strategy; German and American negotiators place greater stress on legal aspects; and Soviet negotiators often ask for a whole loaf when they could get half a loaf but then wind up with nothing.

Although Ikle avoids contributing directly to understanding cultural differences in negotiation, his definition of international negotiation is good: "Negotiation is a process in which explicit proposals are put forward ostensibly for the purpose of reaching agreement on an exchange or on the realization of a common interest where conflicting interests are present." Without common interests there is nothing to negotiate for, and without conflict there is nothing to negotiate about.

In *A Behavioral Theory of Labor Negotiations*, Walton and McKersie show that without common and conflicting interests negotiation is pointless because agreement is impossible [23].

Positive Settlement Range

The settlement range can be either positive or negative. If the settlement range is positive, then the resistance points are compatible and a mutually satisfactory agreement can be reached.

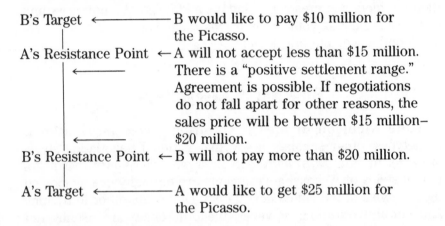

B's Target ←——————— B would like to pay $10 million for the Picasso.

A's Resistance Point ← A will not accept less than $15 million.
There is a "positive settlement range." Agreement is possible. If negotiations do not fall apart for other reasons, the sales price will be between $15 million–$20 million.

B's Resistance Point ← B will not pay more than $20 million.

A's Target ←——————— A would like to get $25 million for the Picasso.

Negative Settlement Range

If the settlement range is negative, then the resistance points are incompatible and a mutually satisfactory agreement cannot be reached. There is no settlement which would be minimally acceptable to both parties.

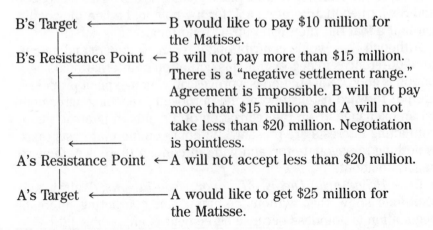

B's Target ←——————— B would like to pay $10 million for the Matisse.

B's Resistance Point ← B will not pay more than $15 million.
There is a "negative settlement range." Agreement is impossible. B will not pay more than $15 million and A will not take less than $20 million. Negotiation is pointless.

A's Resistance Point ← A will not accept less than $20 million.

A's Target ←——————— A would like to get $25 million for the Matisse.

An Early International Negotiation Model

In "Bargaining and Negotiation in International Relations," Jack Sawyer and Harold Guetzkow present a socio-psychological model for analyzing international negotiation. In their model, negotiation is composed of five aspects: (1) *goals*, motivating the parties to enter and sustain (2) the *process* of negotiation itself that involves communications and actions leading to (3) certain *outcomes* for each—all occurring within and influenced by (4) pre-existing *background* factors of cultural traditions and relations between and within parties, and (5) specific situational *conditions* under which the negotiation is conducted [19]. (See Table 6-2.)

Sawyer and Guetzkow recognize that nations may have a "national character" that influences the types of goals and processes a society pursues in negotiation. It is unlikely that the elites who conduct international negotiation are so cosmopolitan that they can shed their national character. Therefore, cultural differences may affect international negotiations in many different ways.

A major area of concern is the attitude negotiators hold towards each other as a result of prior relations between their respective nations. These attitudes are crucial to the outcome of the negotiations. An ethnocentric attitude may consistently lead to negative interpretations of the foreign counterpart's actions. These negative interpretations become self-reinforcing and may result in an emphasis on conflicting interests. Ethnocentrism may result in the conflict spiraling out of control and the negotiations coming to an end.

A Comparative Study of Negotiation Style

Scholars and researchers have developed frameworks for comparative studies of negotiation style. In *Disputes and Negotiations: A Cross-Cultural Perspective*, P.H. Gulliver asserts that the negotiation process is essentially similar around the world despite marked differences in interests, ideas, values, rules, and assumptions among different negotiators in different societies [9].

Gulliver sees negotiation as involving two distinct processes going on simultaneously: (1) a cyclical process of information

Table 6-2
Sawyer/Guetzkow
International Negotiation Model

Antecedent Goals	Concurrent Process	Consequent Outcome
Communality of goals	Preparation for negotiation	Clarity of outcomes
Specificity of goals	Intersection of alternatives and utilities	Criteria for evaluating outcomes
	Modification of utilities: Communication Persuasion	Continuity of alternatives
	Modification of alternatives: Threats and promises Fait accompli Creating new alternatives	

Background Factors	Conditions
Cultural variation	The setting of negotiation: Types of negotiation
Attitude between parties	Open vs. secret diplomacy
Relations within parties	The number of participants
The negotiator: Status and background	The number of parties
Personality	Information: Estimating the other's utilities
	Stresses upon negotiation
	The timing of negotiation

From: "Bargaining and Negotiation in International Relations" in International Relations: A Social-Psychological Analysis Herbert Kelman (ed.) NY: Holt, Rinehart & Winston, 1965.

exchange and learning and (2) a developmental process that moves the negotiation along from its initiation to its conclusion and implementation.

During the cyclical process, negotiations proceed through the exchange of information between the parties, and between them and third parties. Information is verbal and nonverbal, including evidence, argument, appeals to rules and ideology, expressions of strength and proposals of terms for agreement. This exchange permits a learning process by which each party formulates, modifies, and readjusts expectations, preferences, and proposals. In consequence, the parties approach agreement on the outcome.

The developmental process involves successive phases in which the negotiators focus on particular areas. The phases of the developmental process can be summed up as: (1) the search for an arena for the negotiations; (2) the formulation of an agenda and working definitions of the issues in dispute; (3) preliminary statements of demands and offers and the explorations of the dimensions and limits of the issues, with an emphasis on the differences between the parties; (4) the narrowing of differences, agreements on some issues, and the identification of the more obdurate ones; (5) preliminaries to final bargaining; (6) final bargaining; (7) ritual confirmation of the final outcome; and, in many cases, (8) the implementation of the outcome or arrangements for implementation. The phases are not necessarily neatly ordered and sequential in linear, chronological order. Two or three phases may overlap. Negotiators may return to earlier phases to take up previously neglected matters, to clarify others, or to start afresh in light of later experience.

Considerations in Cross-Cultural Negotiation

Glen Fisher presents a framework for analyzing cross-cultural negotiations in *International Negotiation: A Cross-Cultural Perspective*. Fisher addresses five considerations: (1) the players and the situation; (2) styles of decision making; (3) national character; (4) cross-cultural noise; and (5) interpreters and translators. Each consideration presents questions that should be answered before entering international negotiations. Fisher provides broad answers to his questions by examining international negotiations with Japanese, French, and Mexican counterparts [7].

The Players and the Situation

Fisher asserts that a cultural dimension exists in the way negotiators view the negotiation process. This raises several issues. Form, hospitality, and protocol may be important to the success of international negotiations. Difficulties sometimes arise from the different expectations negotiators have regarding the social setting of the negotiation. The negotiator should discover what the foreign negotiator expects and then provide a tension-free environment that encourages cooperation and problem solving.

There also may be a national style in choosing negotiators and in selecting negotiating teams. Negotiators can anticipate a counterpart's behavior by researching biographical data and analyzing the negotiator's organizational or institutional role. In the case of negotiating teams, it is useful to discover how corporate culture affects internal dynamics.

Styles of Decision Making

Fisher contends that patterns exist in the way officials and executives structure their negotiation communication systems and reach institutional decisions. The organizational culture of a foreign corporation may provide formal rules and regulations guiding its decision-making process. A negotiator can find ways to influence a foreign corporation's decisions by analyzing its corporate culture and structuring arguments to fit within established guidelines.

Furthermore, general cultural patterns exist by which individual negotiators develop personal styles of decision-making behavior. By discovering how foreign counterparts look at facts and analyze data, successful negotiators can provide information that will increase the probability of a successful outcome.

National Character

Studies of national character call attention to the patterns of personality that negotiators exhibit and to the collective concerns that give a nation a distinctive outlook in international relationships. Foreign negotiators concerned with international image may be preoccupied with discussions of their national heritage, identity, and language. Cultural attitudes, such as ethnocentrism or xenophilia, may influence the tone of their argument.

Fisher maintains that foreign negotiators display many different styles of logic and reasoning. International negotiators frequently find discussions impeded because the two sides seem to be pursuing different paths of logic. Negotiation breakdown may result from the way issues are conceptualized, the way evidence and new information are used, or the way one point seems to lead to the next.

During the discussions, the foreign counterpart may pay more attention to some arguments than to others. Greater weight may be given to legal precedence, expert opinion, technical data, amity, or reciprocal advantage. A good international negotiator will discover what is persuasive to the foreign counterpart and use that method of persuasion.

Foreign negotiators may place different values on agreements and hold different assumptions as to the way contracts should be honored. The negotiator must find out how the counterpart intends to implement the agreement. A signature on a piece of paper or a handshake may signify friendship rather than the closing of a contract.

Cultural Noise

Noise consists of background distractions that have nothing to do with the substance of the foreign negotiator's message. Factors such as gestures, personal proximity, and office surroundings may unintentionally interfere with communication. The danger of misinterpretation of messages necessitates analysis of various contextual factors.

Interpreters and Translators

Fisher points to limitations in translating certain ideas, concepts, meanings and nuances. Subjective meaning may not come across through words alone. Gestures, tone of voice, cadence, and double entendres are all meant to transmit a message. Yet these are not included in a translation.

Sometimes a negotiator will try to communicate a concept or idea that does not exist in the counterpart's culture. For example, the American and English concept of "fair play" seems to have no exact equivalent in any other language. How then can an Englishman expect "fair play" from a foreign counterpart?

Interpreters and translators may have difficulty in transmitting the logic of key arguments. This is especially true in discussions of abstract concepts such as planning and international strategy. The parties may think that they have come to an agreement, when, in fact, they have entirely different intentions and understandings.

Fisher's five-part framework provides scholars and consultants with a launching pad for both theory building and practical applications.

Practical Advice for International Negotiators

Several good books offering practical advice to international managers are available, and they are listed with the references at the end of this section. In *Going International: How to Make Friends and Deal Effectively in the Global Marketplace,* Copeland and Griggs offer 20 practical rules for international negotiators [6].

COPELAND AND GRIGG'S 20 PRACTICAL RULES FOR INTERNATIONAL NEGOTIATIONS

BEFORE THE NEGOTIATION

Rule 1:   Make sure what you are negotiating is negotiable.

Rule 2:   Define what "winning" the negotiation means to you. Be ambitious but set a realistic walk-away.

Rule 3:   Get the facts.

Rule 4:   Have a strategy for each culture and each phase. First, decide how to position your proposal. Second, decide whether to be competitive (win-lose) or cooperative (win-win). Third, set your opening offer. Fourth, plan to control your concessions.

(continued on next page)

(continued)

Rule 5:   Send a winning team. Don't go alone. Always have your own interpreter. Exclude lawyers and accountants from the negotiating team. In some cases use a go-between. Don't change negotiators in midstream.

Rule 6:   Allow yourself plenty of time, and more. Never tell the other side when you are leaving.

BEGINNING THE NEGOTIATION

Rule 7:   Make the opening scene work for you. Think about the agenda. Watch the physical arrangements. The overture should make music.

HARD BARGAINING

Rule 8:   Control information.

Rule 9:   Watch your language.

Rule 10: Persuasion is an art. Don't paint your argument with the wrong materials. Thinking on the same plane is important. Be wary of the persuasion strategies Americans love.

Rule 11: Get in stride with the locals. Most important: take time out.

Rule 12: Go behind the scenes—that is where minds are changed.

Rule 13: Give face.

Rule 14: A deadlock means neither side wins, but both may lose.

Rule 15: Don't be browbeaten into a bad deal. You must be able to walk away.

Rule 16: Get your agreement signed before you leave.

Rule 17: Both sides should agree on the significance of what you are signing.

Rule 18: Be willing to give up cherished notions of the proper contract.

BEYOND THE CONTRACT

Rule 19: Discussions are always preferable to court settlements.

Rule 20: Remember—without a relationship, you have no deal.

Summary

There is no agreement on one set definition of negotiation; however, there are identifiable characteristics and immutable principles of negotiation that haven't changed for thousands of years. Perhaps the best advice on negotiation comes from Monsieur de Callieres, an eighteenth-century French diplomat. Recommendations include the necessity to study the foreign environment and to make an adequate record of the negotiation.

Scholars have developed comparative models around the universal characteristics of negotiation. One early model by Sir Harold Nicolson identifies two archetypes of international negotiators: warriors (Germans) and shopkeepers (English). Other scholars argue that national negotiating styles are rare, but find commonalities among negotiators from different countries.

Some comparative studies focus on cultures rather than nations. Gulliver looks at negotiating styles in many cultures, including primitive tribes. Other comparative studies are cross-cultural, but emphasize national character. Fisher looks at negotiating styles in the United States, France, Japan, and Mexico. Weiss and Stripp examine negotiating styles in France, Mexico, Japan, the People's Republic of China, Nigeria, and Saudi Arabia. There are also many studies that are country specific, e.g., Moran's book on how to negotiate in Japan.

Negotiators can use existing international negotiation models as tools to manage cultural differences and improve prospects of success. Alternatively, negotiators can build cutomized models that are more appropriate to their unique circumstances.

References and Suggested Readings

1. Bartos, Otomar J. *Process and Outcome of Negotiations.* New York: Columbia University Press, 1974.
2. Bazerman, Max H. and Margaret Neale. "Heuristics in Negotiation: Limitations to Effective Dispute Resolution." in *Negotiating in Organizations.* Max Bazerman and Roy Lewicki (eds.) Beverly Hills: Sage Publications, 1983.
3. Callieres, Francois de. *On the Manner of Negotiating with Princes.* Translated by A.F. Whyte. Notre Dame. Indiana:

University of Notre Dame Press, 1963; Originally published, Paris: Michael Brunet, 1716.

4. Casse, Pierre and S. Deol. *Managing Intercultural Negotiations.* Yarmouth, Maine: Intercultural Press, 1985.

5. Condon, John. *Good Neighbors: Communicating with the Mexicans.* Yarmouth, Maine: Intercultural Press, 1985.

6. Copeland, Lennie and Lewis Griggs. *Going International: How to Make Friends and Deal Effectively in the Global Marketplace.* New York: Random House, 1985.

7. Fisher, Glen. *International Negotiation: A Cross-Cultural Perspective.* Chicago: Intercultural Press, 1980.

8. Graham, John L. and Yoshihiro Sano. *Smart Bargaining: Doing Business with the Japanese.* Cambridge: Ballinger, 1984.

9. Gulliver, P.H. *Disputes and Negotiations: A Cross-Cultural Perspective.* New York: Academic Press, 1979.

10. Ikle, Fred C. *How Nations Negotiate.* New York: Harper & Row, 1964.

11. Lall, Arthur. *Modern International Negotiation.* New York: Columbia University Press, 1966.

12. Lax, David A. and James K. Sebenius. *The Manager as Negotiator.* New York: The Free Press, 1986.

13. Moran, Robert T. *Getting Your Yen's Worth: How to Negotiate with Japan, Inc.,* Houston: Gulf Publishing, 1985.

14. Moran, Robert T. and Philip Harris. *Managing Cultural Synergy.* Houston: Gulf Publishing, 1982.

15. Nicolson, Sir Harold. *Diplomacy.* New York: Oxford University Press, 1964.

16. Nierenberg, Gerard I. *Fundamentals of Negotiating.* New York: Hawthorn Books, 1973.

17. Pruitt, Dean J. *Negotiation Behavior.* New York: Academic Press, 1981.

18. Pye, Lucien. *Chinese Commercial Negotiating Style.* Cambridge: Oelgeschlager, Gunn & Hain, 1982.

19. Sawyer, Jack and Harold Guetzkow. "Bargaining Behavior in International Relations." in *International Relations: A Social-Psychological Analysis.* Herbert C. Kelman (ed.). New York: Holt, Rinehart & Winston, 1965.

20. Sperber, Philip. *The Science of Business Negotiation.* New York: Pilot Books, 1979.

21. Stripp, William G. and Robert Lenberg. "Negotiating with Mexican Businesspersons," 1986.
22. Tung, Rosalie. *Business Negotiations with the Japanese.* Lexington Books, 1984.
23. Walton, Richard E. and Robert B. McKersie. *A Behavioral Theory of Labor Negotiations.* New York: McGraw-Hill, 1965.
24. Weiss, Stephen E. and William G. Stripp. "Negotiating with Foreign Businesspersons." New York: New York University Graduate School of Business Administration monograph #85-9, 1985.

7

....

A FRAMEWORK FOR GLOBAL BUSINESS NEGOTIATIONS

In "Negotiating with Foreign Businesspersons" (1985), Stephen Weiss and William Stripp present a framework for analyzing cross-cultural negotiations. Weiss and Stripp maintain there are 12 variables in every international negotiation that are focal points for cultural impact. Changes have been made in the framework in order to simplify its use.

Framework Overview

The Framework for Global Business Negotiations (1991) was created to help businesspeople win global negotiations. The framework helps negotiators make intelligent decisions and take appropriate actions before, during, and after global negotiations by enabling them to predict and interpret the actions of their foreign counterparts.

The framework distinguishes four components, each representing a key aspect of the negotiation process. The individual components are composed of one or more variables. The variables furnish a comprehensive and useful checklist of factors that a negotiator should consider when preparing for negotiation.

First, the negotiator should conduct an initial research of relevant literature concerning the target culture and, if possible, extensive interviews of individuals who have negotiating experience with the target culture. Businesspeople should then use the framework to organize their research findings. They should analyze the information and develop a set of provisional propositions on the target culture. These provisional propositions should be used in devising plans before the negotiation begins.

When interaction begins, the negotiator may observe deviations from the provisional propositions. The negotiator should not be disturbed by this. The initial research comes from books and other people's experiences. The past experiences of other businesspeople are valuable, but are not always reliable. The negotiator must accept change and be prepared to face unexpected situations.

The framework is a dynamic model and, as interaction occurs, the negotiator should continually add personal observations and adjust the propositions accordingly. In this manner, the negotiator can arrive at a personal understanding of the foreign counterpart's motivations, needs, perspectives, and expectations.

The framework is particularly well-suited for computer applications. The provisional propositions can be organized and stored on diskette. Using compact and laptop computers, the propositions can be reviewed and modified while flying overseas, in a foreign hotel room, and even throughout the actual negotiation process. In this manner, an individual or organization can build a personalized library that combines general information and personal observations on negotiating with specific cultures, organizations, and individuals. The library will then be available for future reference, providing a catalogued history of past global negotiations.

The framework is easy to understand and use. Its basic form can be adapted and changed as the situation and environment change. Negotiators should customize the framework to suit their own purposes.

The Components

Negotiation is a cyclical process of policy formulation, interaction, deliberation, and outcome. Figure 7-1 shows an example of this process using Company A from the United States that wants to enter an alliance with Company B from Japan. The companies have agreed to enter into negotiations. In preparing for the negotiations, A wants to answer the following questions about B: **Policy**—What is B's philosophy of negotiation? How does B choose its negotiators? What does B want? How will the negotiators act? **Interaction**—How will B's negotiators try to persuade us? What forms of nonverbal communication will be used? How will B's negotiators organize time? **Deliberation**—How can we get B's negotiators to trust us? Are they willing to take risks? On what will they base their decisions? **Outcome**—How can we reach an agreement?

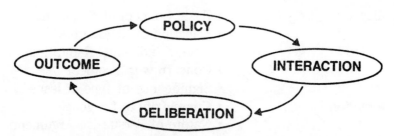

Figure 7-1. Global negotiations flowchart.

"Policy" defines the vital interests of a business and describes the customary course of action used to protect and promote those interests. In world trade and investment, businesses have three broad policy alternatives: isolation in the domestic market, competition on a global scale, or cooperation in the creation of strategic alliances. All three choices require cross-cultural negotiation.

"Interaction" is the period of information exchange during which the negotiators propose offers and counteroffers. The process of interaction is a continual stream of acts, words, and gestures that are intended to persuade the counterpart. The flow of information permits each party to learn about the counterpart's expectations.

"Deliberation" is the process by which the negotiators evaluate the interaction, adjust their understanding of the counterpart's requirements, and reformulate expectations, preferences and proposals in an effort to resolve conflicting interests.

"Outcome" refers to the final understanding reached by the parties. The negotiators may come to some agreement or may conclude that agreement is impossible. Sometimes, negotiations do not have a definitive ending and either continue on or are put off indefinitely. Whatever the outcome, it will cause the business to evaluate its policy.

The Variables

The Framework for Global Business Negotiations divides the four components into twelve variables that can influence the success or failure of global negotiations:

1. Policy
   - Basic Concept of Negotiation
   - Selection of Negotiators
   - Role of Individual Aspirations
   - Concern with Protocol
   - Significance of Type of Issue
2. Interaction
   - Complexity of Language
   - Nature of Persuasive Argument
   - Value of Time
3. Deliberation
   - Bases of Trust
   - Risk-Taking Propensity
   - Internal Decision-Making Systems
4. Outcome
   - Form of Satisfactory Agreement

By selectively categorizing information under each of these twelve variables, negotiators can develop a profile that will show the counterpart's philosophy of negotiation; who the negotiators are and why they were selected; what the negotiators want for themselves; how they will act and how they will expect others to act; what kind of things are most important to them; how they try to persuade others verbally and nonverbally; how they use time and how long they expect negotiations to take; what makes them trust someone; how they handle risk; who makes the decisions and how the decisions are made; and what form of agreement they expect. (See Table 7-1.)

In customizing the framework to suit their individual needs, negotiators may want to add or subtract certain variables.

Table 7-1
Framework for Global Business Negotiations (1991)

Variables	Negotiator's Profile	
1. Basic Concept of Negotiation	strategic ⟷	synergistic
2. Selection of Negotiators	technical ability ⟷	social skills
3. Role of Individual Aspirations	organization ⟷	self
4. Concern with Protocol	formal ⟷	informal
5. Significance of Type of Issue	substantive ⟷	relationship-based
6. Complexity of Language	verbal ⟷	nonverbal
7. Nature of Persuasive Argument	logic ⟷ dogma	emotion
8. Value of Time	strict ⟷	relaxed
9. Bases of Trust	law ⟷	friendship
10. Risk-Taking Propensity	cautious ⟷	adventurous
11. Internal Decision-Making Systems	authoritative ⟷	consensus
12. Form of Satisfactory Agreement	explicit ⟷	implicit

Basic Concept of Negotiation

Although negotiation has universal aspects, negotiators are driven by a variety of different beliefs, concepts, and attitudes regarding proper approaches to the negotiation process. Depending upon custom, tradition, and/or personal preference, a negotiator will use diverse procedures, techniques, and methods of inquiry to obtain the desired ends. There are two basic opposing philosophies of negotiation: strategic and synergistic.

Basic Concept of Negotiation

Strategic	Synergistic
Purpose:	
• Maximization of individual benefit	• Maximization of joint benefit
Beliefs:	
• Zero-sum	• Nonzero-sum
• Conflict is functional	• Conflict is dysfunctional
• Opposing interests are illegitimate	• Opposing interests are legitimate
• To solve conflict must coerce other	• To solve conflict must work together
Attitude:	
• Competitive	• Cooperative
• Suspicious	• Trusting
• Hostile	• Friendly
• Ready to exploit other's needs	• Ready to respond helpfully
• Sensitive to differences	• Sensitive to common interests
Communication:	
• Misleading	• Open and honest
• Confrontational	• Nonconfrontational
• Expands scope of conflict	• Limits scope of conflict
• Stimulates a sense of opposition	• Stimulates conformity and convergence of beliefs and values

Under the strategic negotiation model, resources are seen to be limited, i.e., there is a fixed pie. Each side wants to get as much of the pie as it can get; however, if one party gets more, then the other party gets less. As interests are seen to be diametrically opposed, the sides are extremely competitive, often relying on trickery and coercion to obtain desired ends.

Under the synergistic negotiation model, resources are seen to be unlimited, i.e., there is plenty of pie for everyone. Each side wants to get as much pie as it can get and, by cooperating, everyone can have as much as they want. Followers of this model believe that there are several alternative ways in which the parties can obtain their desired ends without one party profiting at the expense of or interfering with the other.

Under the strategic synergy model, there are several types of resources, some are limited and others are unlimited, i.e., there are many kinds of pie, some are plentiful and some are scarce. Each side has differing tastes, but wants as much of the pies that it likes as it can get. Depending upon the situation, followers of this model will use either a strategic or a synergistic approach.

If a negotiator has no knowledge of the counterpart's philosophy of negotiation, then many contingencies must be prepared for and planning becomes overly complex. By determining the counterpart's philosophy, the negotiator can concentrate upon developing specific plans that are appropriate to the counterpart's dispositions. Careful planning based on sound information of the counterpart will lead to an early and favorable agreement.

Selection of Negotiators

A basic fact about negotiation is that foreign negotiators are not abstract representatives of the other side. They are human beings. They have emotions, deeply held values, and different backgrounds and viewpoints. This human aspect of negotiation can be either helpful or disastrous [4].

Variations in prior experience, background, and outlook can affect the negotiator's manner and effectiveness. Individual differences in background (such as sex, age, political affiliation, and social class) as well as individual differences in personality (such as cooperativeness, authoritarianism, and risk-taking propensity) may shape the course of the negotiations. Therefore, it is important to know why the foreign negotiator was selected [15].

Foreign businesses attempt to choose negotiators who are the most capable of achieving satisfactory performance. In practice this means that most negotiator selection decisions are informal and reflect certain biases or preferences. Selection criteria can be broadly categorized under technical ability or social skills. (See Table 7-2.)

Table 7-2
Selection of Negotiators

Technical Ability	←——————————————→	Social Skills
• Achievement		• Ascription
• Scientific skills		• Status
• Legal training		• Personal Attributes
• General knowledge		• Kinship
• Language fluency		• Social class

The number of negotiators considered appropriate for a negotiation appears to vary by culture. In some cases, a negotiating team will include some individuals who are socially skilled and others who are technically adept.

Technical ability is knowledge and proven ability in a particular field of expertise. Individuals who are technically skilled must have proven their ability through reputation, records of success, and demonstration of recognized skills. Negotiating skill and experience are included in this category. Also included are cross-cultural skills, such as ability to learn new customs and procedures and ability to improvise.

Businesses that value technical attributes attempt to make appointments and promotions "scientifically." Negotiators are chosen on the basis of measured competence. Desired characteristics include technical knowledge, scientific skills, language fluency, and legal training.

Businesses that value social skills make appointments and promotions on the basis of social criteria. Desired characteristics include personal attributes and status. Personal attributes are individual characteristics, such as affability, demonstrated loyalty, and perceived trustworthiness. Status is the candidate's relative rank in a hierarchy of prestige. This category includes seniority, political affiliation, social class, sex, age, ethnic ties, kinship and physical characteristics.

Role of Individual Aspirations

The personal ambitions of negotiators are rarely identical with the interests of their corporations. In some cases, the position taken by a foreign negotiator may reflect personal goals to a greater degree than corporate goals. For example, an interest in personal success may lead negotiators to accept terms that are not favorable to their corporations. Negotiators have even been known to act as mediators between the two sides instead of as advocates for their corporations [8].

On the other hand, negotiators may want to prove that they are hard bargainers and decide to cling to a position more stubbornly than is either required by corporate instructions or warranted by any prospects that the counterpart might yield. Personal reputation may be more important than organizational reputation or success of the negotiation.

Like all human beings, negotiators have needs that they want to satisfy. Classical economic theory assumes that, as an individual, the negotiator will act in a manner that best fulfills his interests. This is deceptive in that "his" may refer to several different entities. In the extreme, "his" refers solely to the individual. Often, however, "his" may refer to the individual's family or household, and it is this entity whose interest is being maximized. In other cases, individuals act as if "his" referred to an even larger entity. They appear to act in terms, not of their own interest, but of a larger collectivity or community. They might act in the interest of their profession, their nation, or even the world.

Negotiators are often put in the position of choosing between private goals and corporate goals. The negotiator may resolve this dilemma by exhibiting a "collectivity-orientation" and acting on behalf of the corporation; or the negotiator may exhibit a "self-orientation" and act for personal interests [7 and 13].

The dialectic between aspirations for self and aspirations for community can also be considered in terms of "relational orientation." Kluckhohn and Strodtbeck discuss "individualism," "collaterality," and "lineality." When the individualistic principle is dominant, a negotiator's individual goals have primacy over the goals of the corporation. The negotiator is not allowed to ruthlessly disregard the interests of the corporation; however, it is understood that the negotiator will pursue individual interests along with corporate interests. Negotiators who exhibit a "collateral orientation" strongly identify with their corporations, but lack a strong national consciousness. Negotiators who exhibit a "lineal orientation" identify not only with their corporation, but strongly identify with their nation and history [10].

Concern with Protocol

Protocol lists accepted practices of diplomatic interaction in detailed codes of ceremony and procedure. Ceremony is conventional acts of politeness and etiquette. The underlying principle of ceremony is courteous consideration for the feelings of others, plus recognition of authority and vested responsibility. Procedure is the order to be pursued before, during, and after the negotiation process.

Rules of protocol may be formal or informal. Negotiators who insist on formal protocol stress adherence to strict and detailed rules that govern manners and conduct. They attach importance to explicit displays of courtesy. Parliamentary procedure may be used during the negotiations.

Negotiators who are informal attach little importance to explicit displays of courtesy and are inattentive to rules that govern manners and conduct. Procedure during negotiation does not follow any set rules. Negotiators may constantly interrupt each other.

If the counterpart's expectations of courteous behavior are not met, confusion and unnecessary conflict may result. Failure to follow protocol may be seen as a lack of respect for the counterpart's culture. Seemingly minor slights can cause confusion and conflict. In the extreme, failure to conform to protocol may cause the negotiations to collapse.

Negotiators should give careful attention to the way protocol is applied. It is important to know whether or not the counterpart is using the rules of protocol to either favor or victimize the negotiator. The counterpart may be using protocol to communicate feelings ranging from a desire to see the negotiations successfully concluded to a complete lack of interest. Deliberate breaches of etiquette are often calculated manifestations of distrust.

Site selection is an important aspect of protocol because it affects psychological climate, availability and use of communications channels, and the presence of time limits. When negotiations take place in a foreign land, the host assumes responsibility for arranging the physical space. Physical arrangements, such as the size of tables and the height of chairs, have strategic implications and may become vehicles for accentuating status and power differences. An important political negotiation was held up for months while negotiators argued over the shape of the table.

The rules of protocol govern a variety of activities, including location of the negotiations, welcoming, transportation, official forms of address, presentation of credentials, business and visiting cards, dress codes, gift giving, entertainment, privileges, courtesies, ceremonies, receptions, language, use of interpreters, composition of the negotiating teams, seating arrangements, timing, documentation, departure, and precedence. These activities provide facilities and restraints, encouragements and deterrents to successful negotiation.

Significance of Type of Issue

In negotiation both parties share a common interest. They either want to share the same object or exchange different objects that they cannot gain by themselves, but can only obtain through each other. At the same time, the parties share conflicting interests in that their levels of aspiration (their highest objectives) are incongruent. The term *issue,* means a point arising from, or growing out of, the parties' conflicting interests.

Defining the issues is one of the most important parts of negotiation. Before negotiations begin, each party formulates a preliminary statement of what it sees are the most important issues. The formulation of an issue may stake out the starting points and limits for concessions, fix the benchmarks for evaluating gains and losses, and circumscribe the areas in which pressures, threats and inducements can be used.

This process continues throughout the negotiations. In fact, the negotiators may spend more time in trying to agree what the issues are than in settling them.

An important part of issue definition is determining the counterpart's "vital interests" and "limits." Vital interests are those concerns that the counterpart views as essential to survival, security, or fundamental welfare. Limit is the counterparts' ultimate fallback position, the level of benefit beyond which they are unwilling to concede. If the parties' limits are incongruent, then it is impossible to reach an agreement. (See page 78.)

Negotiators can gain an advantage by analyzing the issues to determine the counterpart's true preferences and priorities. If the negotiators are aware of their counterparts' limit, they can maneuver to get the best possible terms of agreement. At the same time, an understanding of the counterparts' view of the issues will enable negotiators to be more effective in disguising their own preferences and priorities.

Strategic issue analysis in negotiations should concentrate on two types of issues: substantive and relationship-based.

Table 7-3
Significance of Type of Issue

Substantive ⟵——————————⟶ Relationship-based	
• Tangible	• Intangible
• Money	• Personal-internal
• Property	• Values
• Power	• Beliefs

Substantive issues center around control and use of resources, such as space, money, power, property, prestige, and food. All business negotiators want to reach an agreement that satisfies their tangible interests because such interests are the ultimate issue [4].

Relationship-based issues center around the ongoing nature of mutual or reciprocal interests. Most negotiations take place in the context of an ongoing relationship. In an ongoing relationship, it is important to carry on each negotiation in a way that will help rather than hinder future relations and future negotiations. In many situations, the ongoing relationship is more important than the substantive outcome of any single negotiation.

Complexity of Language

"Context" is the vocal and nonvocal aspects of communication that surround a word or passage and clarify its meaning. Contextual aspects of verbal communication include the rate at which one talks; the pitch or tone level of the voice; the intensity or loudness or softness of the speaker's voice; the flexibility or adaptability of the voice to the situation; the variations of rate, pitch and intensity that add effectiveness to delivery; the quality of the voice; fluency; and expressional patterns or nuances of delivery that convey meaning.

Contextual aspects of nonvocal expression include eye contact; pupil contraction and dilation; facial expression; odor; color, including changes in facial tone and match of clothing; hand gestures; body movement; personal distancing; and use of space.

Cultures can be either verbal or nonverbal. In verbal communication, information is transmitted through an elaborated code that makes meanings both explicit and specific. In nonverbal communication, the extra-verbal component of communication is the major channel for transmitting meaning.

Basil Bernstein identifies two general types of code (language) for transmitting messages: restricted code and elaborated code. A restricted code arises when the social relationship is based upon closely shared identifications, upon an extensive range of shared expectations, or upon a range of common assumptions. Thus, a restricted code emerges when the culture raises the "We" above "I" [2].

Common cultural identity reduces the need to explicitly verbalize intent. The extra-verbal component of the communication becomes the major channel for transmitting messages. Meaning comes from how things are said and when they are said, rather than what is said.

The restricted code reinforces the social relationship rather than creating speech that uniquely fits the intentions of the speakers. Restricted codes do not give rise to verbally differentiated "I's." In restricted code, meaning does not have to be fully explicit. A slight shift of pitch or stress, a small gesture, can carry a complete meaning. Communication is accomplished through closely shared identifications and affective empathy that removes the need to elaborate verbal meanings.

An elaborated code arises whenever the culture emphasizes the "I" over the "We," that is, whenever the intent of the other person cannot be taken for granted. Speakers are forced to elaborate their meanings by making them both explicit and specific. Meanings that are limited to the speaker's culture must be eliminated so that the speaker will be understood by the listener.

The elaborated code presupposes a sharp gap between self and others that is crossed through the creation of speech specifically fitting the differentiated "other." As the differentiated other does not share the cultural background of the speaker, the elaborated code helps the speaker make his subjective intent verbally explicit.

In *The Dance of Life* and *Beyond Culture* Edward T. Hall continues Bernstein's discussion of high-context and low-context cultures. High-context or low-context refers to the amount of information that is in a given communication [5 and 6].

Similar to Bernstein's elaborated code, in a low-context communication, information is transmitted through an explicit code to make up for a lack of shared meanings. Hall sees a low-context communication as similar to interacting with a computer. If information is not explicitly stated and the program is not followed completely, then meaning is distorted.

Similar to Bernstein's restricted code, a high-context communication is one in which most of the information is either in the physical context or internalized in the person, while little is in the coded, explicit, transmitted part of the message. High-context communications feature preprogrammed information that is in the receiver and in the setting.

Hall sees high-context communication as faster, more economical, more efficient, and more satisfying than low-context communications; however, if time is not devoted to common programming, then communication is incomplete. For this reason, negotiators should be cautious of becoming involved in high-context communications.

Mushakoji (1976) makes a similar distinction in his description of *erabi* culture and *awase* culture. The *erabi* culture assumes negotiations will proceed via a clear statement of position by each side; therefore, an explicit, standardized vocabulary is used to convey meaning. In contrast, the *awase* culture uses expressions with multifarious nuances that hint at reality rather than describing it precisely. Words are not taken at face value. Rather, meaning must be inferred. In negotiations, the *awase* preference is to infer the counterpart's position without clear explanation [12].

It is important to be aware of nonverbal cues for several reasons. First, the negotiator may unintentionally transmit false messages to the counterpart. Misinterpretation of nonverbal cues may range from feeling that an offer has been made that has not in fact been made to feeling that the negotiations have been ended when they have not in fact been ended. Second, the negotiator may not pick up on or may misinterpret nonverbal cues being transmitted by the counterpart. Third, effective communication may require the use of nonverbal messages. There may be no other acceptable way of communicating.

Nature of Persuasive Argument

Aristotle identified three means of influencing belief and action: *logos* (logical appeal); *pathos* (emotional appeal); and *ethos* (the appeal that comes from the listener's respect for the speaker as a person). In theory, pure argumentation uses only *logos*, or evidence and logical reasoning; however, this is unrealistic, because "logic" is defined subjectively [16].

It is better to think of argumentation in terms of its persuasive ability. Argumentation, then, is the art of persuading others to think or act in a definite way. In ideal form, argumentation unites reasoning with persuasive power. It convinces by adapting the material to the interests, prejudices, and idiosyncrasies of the audience, as well as exciting the emotions to just the extent necessary for the desired ends.

Argumentation in global negotiations involves a blend of logic, emotion, and dogma.

Negotiators who use logic try to persuade their counterparts with "substantive proof." To provide substantive proof, the negotiator must use empirical or factual evidence. Empirical evidence consists of presumably verifiable statements, including statistical reports, cost benefit analyses, and financial statements.

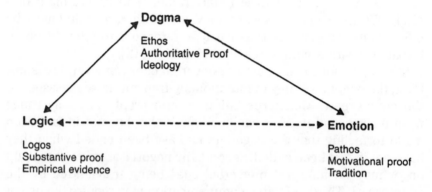

Figure 7-2. Nature of Persuasive Argument.

Negotiators who use emotional appeal try to persuade their counterparts with "motivational proofs." They provide evidence that coincides with the emotions, values, or motives of the counterpart including evidence from historical and cultural tradition.

Negotiators who use dogma try to persuade their counterparts with "authoritative proofs." They provide a statement of opinion from a person whose training and practice qualify him as an authority. This could include dogma from a religious expert, or ideology from a political expert, or even a statement of intuition from a matriarch [3].

The form of proof that negotiators rely on has a direct bearing on the course of negotiation. Dogmatic bargainers make fewer concessions, achieve fewer agreements, take longer to reach an agreement, and are more prone to view compromise as a defeat. By determining what forms of proof counterparts will rely on, global negotiators can increase the attractiveness of proposals by preparing arguments that fit the counterpart's interests, values, and beliefs [14].

Value of Time

Every culture possesses an internal clock based on rhythmic stimuli in specific environments. Cultures can differ in time conception, time perspective, and time experiencing.

All individuals have a preferential orientation toward the past, the present, or the future. The preferred temporal perspective reflects cultural values and provides the foundation for certain forms of negotional behavior [10].

An orientation toward the future implies an expectation of advancement or progressive development. Negotiators are able to predict, plan for, and change forthcoming events and conditions.

An orientation toward the present implies a predominance of the mental state of the moment. The negotiators' only concerns are those that are happening now.

An orientation toward the past implies a belief that everything that is or will be has also existed or taken place in a period before the present.

Temporal perspective influences overall strategy, especially issue formulation and important aspects of decision making. It may be impossible to enter a strict, binding agreement with cultures that have a relaxed perspective of the future.

Cultures have different ways of organizing and using time. Some cultures take a strict view of scheduling and others are more relaxed.

Edward Hall divides cultures into "monochronic" and "polychronic." Monochronic time emphasizes schedules, segmentation and promptness. By scheduling time, monochronic people compartmentalize events and concentrate on one thing at a time. Because scheduling by its nature selects what will be perceived and attended and permits only a limited number of events within a given period, what gets scheduled constitutes a system for setting priorities for both people and functions [6].

Polychronic time stresses involvement of people and completion of transactions rather than adherence to a preset schedule. The future is not solid or firm and, therefore, cannot be planned. Appointments are frequently broken and important plans may be changed right up to the minute of execution.

The organization and use of time can affect the negotiation process and outcome. The level of demands and concessions can be influenced by the amount of time that has elapsed since the beginning of negotiation; therefore, time pressure can be used as a competitive tactic [14].

Bases of Trust

Negotiators face the dilemma of trust. They cannot be completely trusting, because they would be at the mercy of their counterpart's deceptions; however, to believe nothing the counterpart says eliminates the possibility of reaching an agreement [18].

At some point, every negotiator must face the critical problem of having to infer the counterparts' true intentions, interests, and preferences. When the negotiation is governed by mutual trust, the counterparts' behavior can be taken as a true indication of their underlying dispositions. When the negotiation is governed by mutual suspicion, negotiators must develop a "translation" scheme that permits them to decipher what their counterparts really mean [9].

Trust has various meanings. Depending upon theoretical orientation and research interests, trust can be a personality construct, a perception of equitableness and general helpfulness in interpersonal relationships, or a behavior exposing the individual to risky situations.

Trust always implies expectations of some kind, normally having to do with fiduciary obligation and responsibility. In a broad sense, trust can be viewed as expectation of the persistence of the moral social order. In negotiation, trust means reliance upon the accuracy of the counterparts' information and confidence that joint decisions will lead to the desired outcome.

In a broad sense, negotiators base trust on either law or friendship.

Table 7-4
Bases of Trust

Law ←――――――――――――――――――→ Friendship	
• External sanctions provide security	• Relationship provides security
• Droit des gens	• Entente cordiale
• Jus gentium	• Camaraderie
• Punishment for deviant behavior	• Reward for desirable behavior

Trust is sometimes based upon written laws that establish codes of conduct. If an agreement is breached, negotiators who rely upon the law will look to some higher authority to impose sanctions or force performance.

Trust can also be based upon friendship, mutual affection, and esteem. Negotiators rely upon the friendly, harmonious nature of the relationship to ensure that expectations will be fulfilled.

In global business, negotiators usually do not rely on sanctions supported by a higher authority because most international laws are unenforceable. Trust is placed on the counterparts' promises for two main reasons. First, as long as the counterparts find the agreement attractive on balance, they will want to keep their part of the bargain; otherwise, they will not get what they want. Second, corporations have a certain interest in keeping agreements as a matter of principle. If they violate an agreement, they may find it more difficult to reach agreements with other corporations in the future [8].

Risk-Taking Propensity

Decisions can be made under conditions of certainty, risk, or uncertainty. If a decision invariably leads to a specific outcome, then there is "certainty." If a decision leads to one of a set of possible specific outcomes, each occurring with a known probability, then there is "risk." If a decision leads to a set of possible specific outcomes with unknown or unmeaningful probabilities, then there is "uncertainty."

Risk implies the chance of injury, damage, or loss compared to some previous standard. Negotiators are subject to several kinds of loss including "image loss" in the eyes of other negotiators, present and future; "position loss"—the negotiator can't move back after making concessions; "information loss"— opponents can use candid information against the negotiator; and the loss of opportunity for competitive behavior [14].

Generally, negotiators can be labeled either "cautious" or "adventurous." If the negotiator chooses a strategy that offers lower rewards but has a higher probability of success, the negotiator is cautious. If the negotiator chooses a strategy that offers higher rewards but has a lower probability of success, the negotiator is adventurous.

"Uncertainty" implies a complete lack of knowledge about future outcomes or results. For every possible action a negotiator takes, there is an infinite number of possible specific outcomes. Under uncertainty, the negotiator cannot determine the probabilities of future outcomes, therefore, he cannot meaningfully direct action toward a probable outcome.

Geert Hofstede differentiates between levels of "uncertainty avoidance." Uncertainty avoidance means avoiding ambiguous situations rather than avoiding risk. Uncertainty-avoiding cultures have a need for structure and dogma, not a need for safety. Therefore, they often accept highly risky situations because they are familiar with them [7].

If a negotiator chooses a strategy that provides lower rewards but provides the protection of established traditional institutions, the negotiator is an uncertainty-avoider.

If a negotiator chooses a strategy that offers higher rewards but relies upon a new uncertain relationship, the negotiator is an uncertainty-accepter.

Sometimes a negotiator is willing to negotiate even though potential negative consequences outweigh potential positive consequences. If the negotiator is aware of the areas in which the counterpart is willing to risk loss, there is an improved chance of developing satisfactory, innovative solutions.

Internal Decision-Making Systems

In global business negotiations, decisions are made on the basis of past company experience, existing company structure, quality of the international communications system, and personal biases.

Internal decision-making systems can be broadly dichotomized as either "authoritative" or "consensus." In authoritative decision-making systems, leaders or other powerful individuals make decisions without much concern for consensus. Decision-making power is not delegated to the entire negotiating team. The team leader may be given the authority to make a decision without consulting with superiors; however, top management may reserve the right to overrule the team leader's decision.

In consensus decision-making systems, negotiators do not have the authority to make decisions without consulting superiors. The team leader must obtain support from team members and listen to their advice. The team may have to submit information to a committee or to a group of committees before any decision can be made.

Sometimes decision-making authority arises outside of the foreign corporation. A foreign government, unions, stockholders, or suppliers may dictate the final decision.

If decision-making authority does not rest within the foreign negotiating team, negotiators must discover who does have decision-making power and formulate their argument to influence that person or persons. In such situations, it may be best to provide reports, charts, computer programs, and videotapes that can be evaluated at corporate headquarters.

If decision-making power rests solely with the foreign team leader, the negotiator can focus persuasive appeals to fit the leader's disposition. It does little good to convince other team members if the leader won't listen to their advice.

If the decision requires unanimous team approval, the pluralistic nature of the team may prolong the decision-making process. Negotiators may have to wait a long time before they receive a final answer.

Above all else, global negotiation is a process of joint decision making. Each party can only obtain what the other is prepared to allow. Because the parties necessarily begin the negotiations with some kind of differences between them, decision making involves a convergence. At least one party, but usually both, must move toward the other. Although there may be compromise of some sort, it is not inevitable since one party may be induced to move altogether to the counterpart's position or, alternatively, there can be a joint, integrative creation of a new position that is acceptable to both parties.

Form of Satisfactory Agreement

Negotiations are entered into ostensibly for the purpose of reaching agreement. An agreement is an exchange of conditional promises in which each party declares that it will act in a certain way on condition that the other parties act in accordance with their promises [11].

Promises are only *manifestations of intention* to act or refrain from acting in a certain way, so a promise is less than absolute. Depending upon the individuals and cultures involved, promise breaking is tolerated, expected and, in certain cases, desired.

The fact that promises are less than absolute has severe implications for the negotiator. A promise projects exchange into the future. If the negotiator's organization takes action in anticipation of performance by the counterpart, nonperformance may cause extreme damage.

To avoid expensive complications, the negotiator must ensure a means of communication understandable to the parties that will lead to a mutually acceptable agreement with an effective mechanism to enforce promises.

There are two broad forms of satisfactory agreement. One is an explicit, detailed written contract that, by covering all contingencies, requires no future cooperation and binds the parties through an outside enforcement mechanism. The other is an implicit, broad oral agreement that, in accepting unforeseen change as normal, leaves room for the parties to deal with the problem and binds them through the quality of their personal relationship.

Table 7-5

Form of Satisfactory Agreement	
Explicit ←	→ **Implicit**

Relationship of the Parties

• Not dependent on identity	• Heavily dependent
• Limited to substance	• Unlimited
• Transferable	• Nontransferable
• Solely the participants	• Participants and their cultures
• No solidarity except through external enforcement agency	• Solidarity from personal relations and cultural support

Communication

• Limited	• Extensive
• Verbal	• Verbal and Nonverbal
• Formal	• Formal and Informal

Exchange of Promises

• Specific terms	• Vague terms
• Carefully laid out obligations	• Ill-defined obligations
• Detailed	• Diffuse
• Measurable	• Unmeasurable
• Breaches are clear	• Breaches are unclear
• No further negotiations are necessary	• As future unfolds adjustments will have to be made

Performance

• Future can be predicted and included in contract	• Cannot be predicted and included in contract
• Everything happens quickly	• Slowly
• Agreement begins and ends clearly	• No sharp commencement; no clear ending
• No future relationship or cooperation is required	• Future cooperation is required

(continued on next page)

(continued)

Duties

• Duty to self	• Duty to both
• Benefit and burden are sharply divided	• Joint burden for joint benefit
• Conflict of interest is accepted	• Conflict of interest is muted
• Belief that selfishness is inherent in exchange	• Belief in cooperation
• If trouble occurs every man for himself	• If trouble occurs deal with it together

---

In its purest form, an explicit contract assumes that no relationship exists between the parties apart from the substantive exchange; however, every business contract involves relations apart from the substantive exchange.

An implicit agreement assumes that the importance of the relationship overrides purely substantive concerns; however, the purpose of business negotiation is to reach an agreement that satisfies substantive interests.

As every agreement involves both substantive and relational elements, no agreement can ever be purely explicit or implicit. Nevertheless, it is important to know what elements form the basis of both pure forms, so that the negotiator can determine what proportions of the explicit/implicit mix will be most satisfactory under the circumstances.

In determining which form of agreement is most desirable, the elements of concern are the relationship of the parties; the communication styles of the parties; the exchange of promises; and performance of the agreement.

Explicit agreements depend heavily upon substantive concerns. Personal relationships are unnecessary and friendship may be a hindrance. The participants are solely concerned with the material satisfactions involved in the substantive exchange. Participants believe that selfishness is an inherent part of exchange and that their only duty is to themselves. Communication is limited, covering only substantive issues. Communicative style is formal, relying heavily upon technical language.

As the participants in explicit agreements try to maximize personal gain, obligations are limited to those specific, detailed actions that lead the counterpart to provide the agreed upon material satisfaction. Therefore, elements of the agreement must be carefully measured and specified.

Explicit agreements depend upon the specific, written details of a contract, that are enforceable by a powerful, external agency. Although circumstances may change, the obligations of the participants do not and each is bound to his explicit commitment. If a participant gets into trouble, the problem is his and his alone. The explicit terms make any breach completely clear, and the contract will be ruthlessly enforced by the external agency regardless of the consequences.

Negotiations never result in purely explicit forms of agreement. Important issues are often settled through tacit understandings that are laid out in ambiguous terms; however, from a strategic perspective, the negotiator wants to explicitly bind the counterpart, while leaving the home organization free of detailed commitments.

In the purest form, implicit agreements depend heavily upon the relationship of the parties. The relationship is not limited to the substance of the negotiation, but achieves solidarity from well-established understandings. The friendly personal relationship that develops is necessary for successful agreement.

As a result, the participants are more concerned with their complex personal noneconomic satisfactions than with the material satisfaction involved in substantive exchange. Participants are personally committed to each other. They believe that joint cooperation for joint benefit is integral to successful exchange.

Communication is extensive, covering subjects apart from the substantive concerns of the negotiations. Communications are formal and informal and the participants rely upon verbal and nonverbal cues to transmit meaning.

As the parties are committed to joint cooperation for joint benefit, obligations are unlimited and, therefore, unmeasurable. The future cannot be foreseen or included in the agreement. Trouble is expected; therefore, promises are expressed in vague terms to leave room for maneuverability.

The long-term nature of the participant's relationship slows everything down. The negotiation process is long and drawn out. Great periods of time may elapse between agreement and performance.

While specific performance is not required, satisfactory performance is assured because of each participant's commitment to the other. As the future changes and trouble arises, the parties will deal with it together.

Implicit agreements hold inherent dangers for the negotiator. First, the parties may conclude the negotiations, unaware that their interpretations of the implicit parts of their agreement are in conflict. Second, there is the risk of deliberate violation, in which one party violates what it knows the other party thought was a mutual —though tacit or unwritten—understanding as to how the implicit guidelines were to be carried out.

Cultures that favor explicit agreements argue that disputes concerning specificity are essentially a symptom of disagreement about substance, not the form, of the agreement. If the counterparts agree on a bargain they wish to conclude, there should be little objection to spelling it out in detail. By refusing to have an agreement recorded in detail, one side indicates that agreement on these points, in fact, does not exist [8].

Explicit agreements, on the other hand, may be too rigid and impersonal to be effective cross-culturally. The lack of social commitment results in an over reliance on an external authority that often does not have the international power to extend effective sanctions in case of a violation of the agreement.

References and Suggested Readings

1. Aristotle. *The Rhetoric.* Edited and translated by Lane Cooper. NY: Appleton-Century-Crofts, 1960.
2. Bernstein, B. *Class, Codes and Control.* NY: Schocken Books, 1975.
3. Ehninger, D. & W. Brockriede. *Decision by Debate.* NY: Dodd, Mead & Co., 1963.
4. Fisher, R. & W. Ury. *Getting To Yes.* NY: Penguin, 1984.
5. Hall, E. *The Dance of Life.* Garden City, NY: Anchor Books, 1984.
6. ———. *Beyond Culture.* Garden City, NY: Anchor Books, 1977.
7. Hofstede, G. *Culture's Consequences.* Beverly Hills: Sage, 1984.

8. Ikle, F. *How Nations Negotiate.* NY: Harper & Row, 1964.

9. Kelley, H. H. "A Classroom Study of the Dilemmas in Interpersonal Negotiation." in K. Archibald (ed.) *Strategic Interaction and Conflict: Original Papers and Discussion.* Berkeley, Ca.: Institute of Int'l Studies, 1966.

10. Kluckhohn, F. & F. Strodtbeck. *Variations in Value Orientations.* Evanston, Ill.: Row, Peterson and Co., 1961.

11. Macneil, I. *The New Social Contract.* New Haven, Conn.: Yale, 1980.

12. Mushakoji, Kinhide. "The Cultural Premises of Japanese Diplomacy." in *The Silent Power: Japan's Identity and the World Role.* Tokyo: Simul Press, 1976.

13. Parsons, T. & E. Shils. *Toward a General Theory of Action.* NY: Harper & Row, 1965.

14. Pruitt, D. *Negotiation Behavior.* NY: Academic Press, 1981.

15. Rubin, J. & B. Brown. *The Social Psychology of Bargaining and Negotiation.* NY: Academic Press, 1975.

16. Thompson, W. *Modern Argumentation and Debate.* NY: Harper & Row, 1971.

17. Weiss, Stephen E. and William G. Stripp. *Negotiating with Foreign Businesspersons.* New York: New York University Graduate School of Business Administration monograph #85-9, 1985.

18. Zartman, I. W. & M. Berman. *The Practical Negotiator.* New Haven: Yale, 1982.

8
....

NEGOTIATING IN JAPAN

Introduction

Through newspapers, radio and television, Americans are bombarded with news of Japan. Despite the abundance of information, Americans remain puzzled by the Japanese. On the one hand, Japan represents everything that is modern: high technology, high fashion, and every time-saving or recreational gadget imaginable. On the other hand, Japan conjures up images of traditional values: hard work, duty to the family and country, and humility. In business negotiations, the misconception of the inscrutable Japanese businessman has caused many lost opportunities.

Historical Perspective

The Japanese people inhabited their homeland for at least 6,000 years. Their culture was affected by the Buddhist missionaries who influenced many of their basic assumptions about life. These assumptions include the value of harmony in society and the collective aspect of the social order. Hence, the overall goal of the Japanese now, as in the past, in social and business situations, is harmony and accord with people and with nature.

Until the nineteenth century, Japan was virtually isolated from the West. The treacherous seas surrounding the islands and the isolationist policies of Japanese rulers kept foreign traders and invaders from entering Japan. These conditions also prevented citizens from leaving. The lack of outside influence produced cultural and behavioral norms that are by their homogeneous nature unique.

The mountainous geography and the importance of rice cultivation fostered a society that was tightly organized. Because of the many mountain ranges, only ten percent of the land can be cultivated, making Japan one of the most densely populated countries in the world. Furthermore, rice cultivation is labor intensive and complex and requires a group effort, encouraging grouping by families and friends. Japanese society was founded on the extended patriarchal familial system. A clan structure formed because authority flowed from a senior male to other male heads of related families. In medieval times, during years of chaos and war, this structure guaranteed certain family members physical and psychology safety. Being Japanese means being a member of an extended family unit.

Ie and *amae* are two characteristics of Japanese culture that have affected their corporate organization. *Ie* concerns the relationship of those outside the immediate family. It is characterized by male dominance, female submission, and general respect for the elderly. *Amae* is the desire for security. The self is immolated for the security and protection of the group. Through *amae*, Japanese society has become group-conscious and strives for the ideals of harmony and unanimity.

The samurai (warrior caste) played a role in the corporate organization. As the constant internal warfare of innumerable power struggles subsided, some samurai members were chosen for less violent roles as administrators of feudal estates.

During the Tokugawa Shogunate of the sixteenth century, a lucrative trade arose between China and Korea. Members of the samurai class became business entrepreneurs crowding out independent village traders.

During the Meiji Era of the nineteenth century, which finally opened Japan to the Western world, the samurai was often the first student of Western culture. Samurai family enterprises developed into major business cartels, known as *zaibatsu*. After World War II the *zaibatsu* were disallowed, but they continued to function as powerful influences in Japanese business and commerce.

Militarily, the Japanese became a superpower by the mid-nineteenth century. In less than one hundred years, Japan occupied the island of Formosa and part of Southeast Asia, annexed Korea, invaded China and fought wars with Russia and the Allies in World War II. Despite increased contact with the outside world, Japan absorbed little of other cultures and left only a small cultural mark on the countries it occupied.

In August 1945, the atomic bomb exploded on Nagasaki and Hiroshima, destroying the land, Japanese psyche, and the cultural seclusion Japan had known for centuries. General MacArthur and the Americans, having defeated Japan, came back to help rebuild it, leaving a great deal of Western culture in the process. Not even an atomic bomb could destroy thousands of years of history, however. Japan adapted certain elements of Western culture to its particular needs, while maintaining its unique cultural identity.

The Western business organization fit well into the familial Japanese model for the harmony of the group. Management took a paternalistic approach towards personnel. The skilled male worker was rewarded with the security of lifetime employment, and promotion was based upon seniority within the organization.

In the 1990s, cultural diffusion is the norm. Indeed, it appears that a global culture is developing. The Japanese eat McDonald's hamburgers; Americans eat sushi.

The Twelve Negotiating Variables

Basic Concept of the Negotiation Process

The Japanese negotiation process is based on the importance of maintaining harmony in relationships. Norms are established concerning obligations to others, benevolence, and the importance of others' attitudes. Application of this ideal precludes open conflict. An inferior is expected to defer automatically to his superior. The ideal way to resolve conflict is through harmonious cooperation coupled with the "warrior ethic" of assertiveness and persistence in negotiation.

If negotiation is based on harmony, a formal setting with each party advocating its own position becomes undesirable. Unplanned compromise, submission to threats, admission of inconsistencies, and other such possibilities make it a face-threatening event. Instead, the Japanese see negotiation as a fluid irrational process, calling for diligent preparation. Instead of addressing issues directly and openly stating positions and counterproposals, they prefer to infer the other parties' assessment of the situation.

The Japanese often repeat previously stated positions, using highly ambiguous language and appear to be inconsistent. The goal of this process is a just, fair, and proper deal and, more generally, a long-term harmonious relationship with their counterparts and their corporations.

Selection of Negotiators

To become a Japanese negotiator, one must have reached a certain level of status and have personal connections to individuals, a university affiliation, or a corporation. Status is judged on an individual's age, seniority, and knowledge. In business, the company's name is more prestigious than an important title.

The negotiating team is usually male, with one member serving as the symbolic head. There are five positions within the team. The first is filled by the individual who introduces the parties initially and facilitates the signing ceremony. The other four places are filled by the operational staff, the middle managers, the chief executive officer, and a mediator for any disputes.

The qualities admired and sought in Japanese negotiators include commitment, persistence, ability to gain respect, credibility, good listening skills, pragmatism, and a broad perspective.

Role of Individual Aspirations

"The protruding nail is hammered down." This adage describes the collective sense of the Japanese culture and alludes to the lack of individual aspirations. Collectivism is the quintessential trait of the Japanese. An American may say, "I did it," but his Japanese counterpart will say, "We did it." A successful negotiation reflects the efforts of the Japanese team, versus the American mindset of an individual's efforts. Many believe this collective sense is the reason for Japan's economic success.

In a recent advertising campaign, Sony gave a slightly different twist to this old adage by stating, "It is said that a protruding nail is struck on the head. But it is such people that Sony needs. We are seeking protruding people." In business and government, the Japanese are beginning to examine the constrictive features of their collective nature and to consider the need for a more creative spontaneous environment.

Concern with Protocol

One should come to Japanese negotiations with formal politeness, conservative conduct, and good manners. Three levels of formality can be found, the highest is used for important strangers (first business meetings) or those who must be shown a high degree of respect. A slightly less formal politeness is used for daily interactions, once negotiations have begun, or between peers. A visitor can observe the least amount of formality between friends. Sensitivity to these different levels will increase a negotiator's effectiveness.

All meetings are opened and closed with some formality. A standing bow, often together with the handshake, is used to greet and say good-by to foreigners.

An intermediary or go-between will usually arrange the initial meeting. If the foreign business person is negotiating alone, he should have a letter of introduction stating his authority to negotiate for a corporation.

Business cards are exchanged at the first formal meeting session. Business cards should be bilingual, Japanese on one side, English on the other. The card is presented with a bow, or nod, and is used by the Japanese to determine status, and to guide their conduct.

A Japanese businessman is rarely addressed by his first name. People are usually referred to by title. The Japanese are not comfortable with the American style of casually addressing others by their first names soon after introduction.

The senior negotiator on a Japanese team generally sits in the middle of his team on one side of the table, rather than at the head.

Those who have authority to make a deal sit to his immediate left and right; those with lesser roles sit at the two ends.

Entertaining and social occasions are an integral part of business life. Japanese negotiators view this as an opportunity to know their counterparts in depth, leaving the detailed discussions of business for the business day. Wives do not generally accompany their husbands unless specifically invited.

Significance of Type of Issue

The Japanese concentrate on relationship-based issues. Trusting interpersonal relationships is as important to the Japanese as favorable business terms. The sincerity and good intentions established with the counterparts are considered relevant to the harmonious outcome of the negotiation.

The Japanese tend to offer a proposal that approximates their needs and often resist adjusting it. They offer what they feel is correct, proper, and reasonable.

A deliberate proposal-counterproposal approach tends to be difficult for the Japanese because consensus is built into their team.

Complexity of Language

Communication in Japan is reserved and self-controlled, with the Japanese relying on indirection and reading between the lines. The context of communication is highly complex. The Japanese consider the spoken word to be only one part of the total picture and the message may convey several levels of meaning. One level, the true meaning, may be quite contradictory to the literal meaning of the words. The language is subtle and complex, and emphasis on a syllable or vowel can change the entire meaning of the word. Much in Japanese culture is understood without the use of words because the culture is so homogeneous.

Negotiators from low context cultures may say what they mean and expect the same in return only to find that the Japanese respond in a countless variety of ways. Foreigners often fail to understand the meaning underneath the word, or the non-verbal cues such as markedly less eye contact and more silence. The emphasis in the United States is on making oneself understood; the emphasis in Japan is on understanding where the other person is coming from.

The Japanese distinguish between what is said publicly (*tatemae,* meaning "truthful") and what they think privately (*honne,* meaning "true mind"). Because Japanese rarely express negative thoughts or answer "no," it is vital that a negotiator ask questions to determine their exact viewpoint.

Nature of Persuasive Argument

The idea of persuasion seems to run against the Japanese grain. They look with horror on the confrontation and debate that can take place in negotiations and would prefer to work behind the scenes where neither party is in danger of losing face.

They place more emphasis on exchanging extensive detailed information. Exposition, rather than argument, may characterize their negotiations. The Japanese see the negotiation as the ritualistic enactment of a predetermined agreement in which intuition, experience and emotional sensitivity are valued. For them, the logical, cognitive, and intellectual approach is insufficient without consideration for the emotional level of the relationships involved.

Value of Time

Time is viewed more subjectively by the Japanese than their Western counterparts. A meeting that might take three days to conclude in the West will probably take two weeks in Japan. Not being hasty is a sign of wisdom and sincerity.

Conversely, the Japanese can be incredibly efficient and aware of critical deadlines. They often make no concession to subjective time and tend to be punctual. Their view of time is both polychronic and monochronic. They have a long time horizon and believe that some factors such as nature and circumstances are not within their control.

Bases of Trust

Bound by cultural traditions, the Japanese make life-long commitments. When entering a business enterprise or negotiation, they foresee a long-lived involvement. Because of this attitude, they develop a high level of trust for their counterparts. They consider entertaining at night after business a way to learn about the personality, character, and trustworthiness of individuals and the companies they represent. Mutual trust and respect matter a great deal. In first time negotiations, an attempt is made to deal with small issues singly, to test the counterparts' reactions. Trust has to be developed, and often comes slowly, but its rewards are great in easing and facilitating the negotiating process.

Risk-Taking Propensity

In general, the Japanese seem averse to uncertainty and risks. Risk avoidance *(kiken kaihi)* is a key principle in Japanese diplomacy and bargaining. The need to save face and not be a failure in a negotiating process are paramount considerations that further their propensity to be low-risk takers.

Internal Decision-Making Systems

The *ringi seido* or consensus in decision making is the style in Japan. Before action is taken, much time is spent with relevant department heads defining the question, seeking their approval, and gathering sufficient information for a plan. An informal agreement is then reached and a formal document of request that outlines the plan is drawn up and sent to several managers for their approval. The plan then goes to top management for the final go-ahead. By this point, to decide is to implement. This system is referred to as "bottom up" planning. Once a decision has been reached, which usually takes considerable time and patience, the Japanese rapidly implement it.

Form of Satisfactory Agreement

The Japanese tend to prefer brief, written agreements that set forth basic principles, but a gentlemen's agreement often has even more force than a legal contract. The latter involves a sense of honor and obligation, two highly regarded elements of Japanese society.

If after signing a contract something goes wrong, the Japanese try to resolve it by mutual agreement. If disputes arise, the common interests of the two parties, or their relative strengths, are factors that generally determine the outcome. Instead of submitting disputes to a third party, such as a court, the Japanese prefer to settle their differences through discussions with the people who are familiar with the respective problems and situations. To submit an issue to court would bring embarrassment to the Japanese. Naturally, there are exceptions to this general statement about business agreements.

Whereas American agreements can run some one hundred pages, Japanese firms keep theirs shorter. The agreement primarily contains comments on the principles that the parties have agreed to use to guide their relationship. Parties may thus respond to any changes in conditions that later occur.

Concluding Scenario
The Japanese Economy: Razor-Sharp?

For the past decade at least, Japanese products have found success in the world's marketplace. The large cash surpluses of Japanese companies have continued to grow. With no sign of this buildup slowing, the number of Japanese investments abroad in manufacturing, real estate, and securities is continuing at a fast pace.

New to their business culture, the Japanese are now learning the art and game of mergers and acquisitions. They began this activity in the United States, then Britain, and are presently moving to Europe. The Japanese approach to mergers and acquisitions is quite simple. First, they buy a minority interest in an organization to get an inside view and gain a degree of influence. As events develop, they expand their minority holding. This strategy gives them quick access to markets, knowledge of technology, and the benefits of diversification.

The Japanese continue to take much of their manufacturing offshore. They do this close to home—in China and countries in Asia—as well as in the United States and Europe. A recent survey by a leading economic magazine in Tokyo estimated that over 3,000 Japanese companies have offshore operations in Asia. There also appears to be a change in attitude from the imperialist tones of the past to a greater willingness to hire and promote local managers and involve host nationals in equity participation. In some cases, these changes were forced by local laws. In others, they were a result of changing Japanese attitudes reflecting a new and longer-term view of their economic presence in an area.

The Japanese continue to have negative opinions about the economic situations in the United States and Europe. Many surveys reveal that the Japanese give Americans low marks for the quality of their products and the effectiveness of their educational system.

But the situation is changing in Japan. After years of pressure, Japanese markets are beginning to open. With rare exceptions, foreign companies are no longer excluded by law or tariff from doing business in Japan. Nevertheless, the market in Japan is still difficult and a great deal of money and patience is required to succeed in it. The Japanese stock market continues to be somewhat erratic, and the political futures of some leading politicians is uncertain. Nevertheless, Japan is expected to be a leader in world economics for many years.

References and Suggested Readings

1. Blaker, Michael. *Japanese International Negotiating Style.* Columbia University Press, 1977.
2. Chambers, Kevin. *The Traveller's Guide to Asian Customs and Manners.* Deephaven, MN: Meadowbrook, Inc., 1988.
3. Condon, John C. *Interact: Japanese and Americans.* Chicago: Intercultural Press, 1983.
4. Condon, John C. *With Respect to the Japanese: A Guide for Americans.* Yarmouth, ME: Intercultural Press, Inc., 1984.

5. Fallow, James. *More Like Us: Making America Great Again.* Houghton Mifflin, 1989.
6. Graham, J.L. and Yoshihino, S. *Smart Bargaining: Doing Business with the Japanese.* Cambridge, MA: Ballinger, 1984.
7. Halberstam, David. *The Reckoning: Made in America or Japan?* New York, NY: William Morrow, 1986.
8. Lanier, Alison R. *The Rising Sun on Main Street: Working With The Japanese.* Morrisville, PA: International Information Associates, 1990.
9. *The Economist Business Traveller's Guide: Japan.* Prentice Hall Press, 1987.
10. Tung, Rosalie. *Business Negotiations With The Japanese.* Lexington Books, 1984.
11. van Wolferen, Karel. *The Enigma of Japanese Power.* Knopf, 1989.

9
·········
NEGOTIATING IN CHINA

Introduction

Despite China's decade-long opening to the outside world, most observers believed China had taken a giant leap backward in June 1989. Troops crushed thousands of unarmed students and protesters, and China's economic and political relationships with many nations were in jeopardy. The confidence of many foreigners who invested billions in helping to modernize China's industrial base had been shaken. Some believed that China had "burned its bridges" with the international business community. But the Chinese are resilient and have begun to reconstruct their relationship with the outside world.

Historical Perspective and Myth of the Chinese Market

The first American perceptions of the Chinese can be traced back to the 1850s when large numbers of Chinese began to arrive in the United States to help fill a labor shortage. Largely centered in California, the Chinese were initially welcomed as "the best immigrants in California," "law-abiding," "inoffensive," "our most orderly and industrious citizens." The Chinese were said to be, "so sober, so obedient, so punctual and reliable that those who employed them would have no other." Mark Twain wrote of the Chinese, "They are a harmless race...They are quiet, peaceable, tractable, free from drunkness, and they are industrious as the day is long. A disorderly Chinaman is rare and a lazy one does not exist..."

Soon, however, resentment began to build. The Chinese were adept employees who were always available, sober, and content with their wages; however, white workers began to hate the Chinese. They were called dangerous, deceitful, vicious, criminal, cowardly, and just all around "inferior from a mental and moral point of view." There were attacks on the Chinese based on cultural, social, economic, religious, physiological, and even biological reasons.

Discriminatory laws were passed against the Chinese, and with these laws came violence. The Chinese were massacred, murdered, robbed, and banished in groups from their living quarters. Their timidity and lack of protest provoked further attacks simply because such characteristics were seen as signs of weakness. The Chinese were deprived of due process of law for protection of their liberty and property, of the right to trial by jury, of being confronted by witnesses, and of having the assistance of council. There was no protection for the victims and no punishment for the crimes. "A Chinaman's chance," came to be a figure of speech for a hopeless situation, one in which a person had a slim chance or none at all. The Chinese were presented as inscrutable, distrustful, crafty, sneaky, devious, unfathomable, backward, savage, and the Yellow Peril.

In ensuing years, American perceptions of the Chinese were influenced by images presented in print and on screen. Charlie Chan was presented as "the inscrutable, mysterious and damned clever Chinaman." Charlie Chan gave way to the funny, but inscrutable, laundrymen of western movies and television serials. The laundrymen gave way to the kung fu experts, culminating in the once-popular TV character Kwai Chang Cain, a half Chinese, half American.

Today many Americans continue to base their perception of the Chinese on their own biases. The Chinese seem to remain as inscrutable as ever.

Misconceptions of China and the Chinese have become prevalent in the West and businesspersons have not escaped the prejudices and the delusions. For over two hundred years, the Chinese market has been seen as an almost limitless market, and to a lesser extent, a vast and as yet untapped source of raw materials.

The Twelve Negotiating Variables

Basic Concept of the Negotiation Process

Early rhetoric emphasizing "friendship and enduring relationships" is quickly overshadowed by distributive bargaining tactics.

A prime consideration for foreigners engaged in business in China is that negotiations may not be negotiations in the Western sense of the word. The Western view of negotiation is best summed up by Ikle: "Negotiation is a process in which explicit proposals are put forward ostensibly for the purpose of reaching agreement on an exchange or on the realization of a common interest where conflicting interests are present." The key word here is ostensibly. Some businessmen naively enter into negotiations with the Chinese under the assumption that their counterparts wish to reach an agreement; however, there are other reasons to enter into pseudonegotiations. Some firms and countries enter into pseudonegotiations with secondary firms for strategic reasons, e.g., they want to get a lower price from the chosen counterpart. Yet another reason is intelligence gathering. A firm or country may have no intention of reaching an agreement, but instead, uses pseudonegotiations to gather information that is unavailable in the home country. The Chinese appear to follow the latter course in some cases.

In business interactions with the Chinese in which there is intent to reach an agreement, the concept of "economic value" is of prime importance. During the negotiations, the relativity of economic value is recognized and justice is achieved in the final balance struck in bargaining.

Although there might be severe cold-hearted bluffing between negotional counterparts, good humor and human heartedness must also exist. The Chinese term for this "man-to-man-ness" is *jen*.

Selection of Negotiators

The Chinese oscillate in selection practices, emphasizing political loyalty during times of turbulence and expertise during times of relative calm.

Traditional Chinese government adopted the attitude that if an official was trained in Confucian virtues, his particular daily actions would be proper. In the People's Republic of China (PRC) today, the government takes the view that cadres should have proper political understanding before they can be correct in their analysis of particular economic problems.

In the 1980s, China recognized its great need for expertise. As Deng said in 1980, "Expert does not mean red, but red requires expert. If you are not expert, and don't know much, but blindly take command...you will only delay production and construction." As a result, concrete measures are being taken to acquire more competent personnel.

This increased emphasis on expertise in no way overshadows the importance of being correct. The overriding consideration of the powers that be in the PRC is to make sure that the bureaucracy and the country remain safely politicized. At all times, political reliability is a must, and this is especially true since the events in May and June of 1989.

Foreigners often find their Chinese counterparts to be well-educated, but lacking in managerial know-how and technical expertise.

Three points about Chinese negotiating teams are important. First, Chinese teams are large, perhaps following Mao's dictum of concentrating a superior force in numbers against the opposition. Second, lawyers are rare. Third, Chinese foreign language specialists are spread so thin that the Chinese team interpreters may have inadequate language skills and experience.

Role of Individual Aspirations

Despite attempts at "cultural remolding," individual aspirations are of paramount importance.

Before the communist revolution, China was seen as a nation of individualists. In 1935, Lin Yutang wrote: "[The Chinese] are family-minded, not social-minded, and the family is only a form of magnified selfishness. The family, with its friends, became a walled castle, with the greatest communistic cooperation and mutual help within, but coldly indifferent toward, and fortified against the world without. In the end, as it worked out, the family became a walled castle outside where everything is legitimate loot." This view of the Chinese as a nation of individualists was also shared by LaBarre who said that money and food were in fact the two foci of the Chinese ellipse.

The "cultural remolding" attempted by Mao and the Communist party tried to eliminate these individualistic tendencies in the Chinese. The most basic assumption of Chinese communism is that being a good member of society, and putting group goals before individual needs, should govern all practices. To reward allegiance to the unit and to the nation as a whole, the concept of sharing predominated. Everyone made sacrifices equally and everyone shared in the relatively meager reward and outcomes. This assumption still exists today. With the opening of China to the West, it is obvious that the individualistic tendencies of the Chinese were not eliminated by Mao's cultural remolding, but merely suppressed.

Concern with Protocol

Playing the host's role to the hilt, the Chinese gather information and hope to gain advantages of surprise and uncertainty in agenda arrangements.

The humanism of the Chinese springs from their concept of the cosmos as "a vast system of behaviors regulated by proto-colar etiquette that is a model for its earthly counterpart." So for the Chinese, etiquette is a religion, a creed based on a complex set of magical relationships. In ancient times, etiquette and ritual were described as "the highest administrative duty, the source of the country's strength." Every Chinese citizen became caught in a fantastic web of rites and obligations that imprisoned him from the cradle to the grave and even fettered his mind. Today the Chinese follow some basic rules of social behavior derived in part from *keqi*, which prescribes polite, courteous, and humble behavior.

Chinese negotiators appreciate the home-court advantages as hosts of determining the procedure and timing of meetings and unilaterally controlling agenda before the actual negotiating sessions. During the initial interactions, much of the preliminary hospitality and exchange of pleasantries is calculated to provide the Chinese with opportunities to size up their counterparts, determining reliability and potential weaknesses.

Significance of Type of Issue

While relationship-based issues receive manifest attention, substantive issues are the driving force for the Chinese.

The Chinese work during the entire negotiation process to establish some form of emotional bond with their counterpart. Jack Shamash, a silk trader, said, "Personal relationships are extremely important in China. Once they know you and you gain their trust, you're a friend of theirs for life, and all doors are unlocked for you without lengthy red tape." The Chinese place a tremendous emphasis on dealing with old friends, *guanxi*. Initially, they use equality and mutual benefit as "hooks," to keep negotiations alive. They then attempt to establish *guanxi* between the counterparts.

What this boils down to is that the Chinese are, in fact, concerned with substantive issues. It is true that the Chinese like to buy from old friends, but it is also true that "old friends" are made after a week or so of meetings.

The Chinese also tend to buy from market leaders and to insist on the best regardless of the appropriateness. While the Chinese want the best, they do not want to pay a premium for it. They believe that bigger companies should be willing to share knowledge at no cost. Also, the Chinese feel that they are especially deserving and should be given discount prices and special considerations.

Complexity of Language

Chinese have a genius for accomplishing their purpose by indirect methods or by the use of conventions that are perfectly understood by them, but puzzling to foreigners.

According to Hall, Hsu, and others, China is a high-context culture and, "It is sheer folly to get seriously involved with high-context cultures unless one is really contexted." This means that every person knows the implicit and unstated values even if they are inexact and imprecise.

The most striking personal characteristic of Chinese negotiators is their ability to separate whatever emotions they may show from the actual progress of the negotiations. Chinese negotiators never telegraph their next moves through displays of emotion.

Nature of Persuasive Argument

The Chinese use a false rhetoric of "no compromise" to establish relative economic value.

The Chinese talk of solidarity, but their methods of argumentation, in the American view, do not promote solidarity. The Chinese affirm dogmatically that their side is right and the other side is wrong.

American negotiators must be careful not to draw hasty conclusions from the rhetoric of no compromise. While rigid statements by Chinese negotiators hint of no middle road, or no third choice, there is considerable scope for compromise.

Value of Time

Traditional Chinese views of time in combination with observed American impatience have led the Chinese to become "masters of the art of stalling."

Time in China has not achieved the abstract qualities it has in the West, and Western observers have never been able to determine whether the Chinese savor time or just disregard it. We do know that the Chinese civilization has been around for thousands of years and the Chinese seem to take a much longer view of time than Americans.

Bases of Trust

Trust, being based on past record, presents problems for Americans who must overcome Chinese xenophobia.

The underlying current of Chinese political and cosmological philosophy is to live with people and get in step with the universe, for people are essentially good and the universe is primarily benevolent. Traditionally, many Chinese agreed with the theory that man's nature is inherently good, but few were willing to go so far as to test it in business dealings. As one author said, "The Chinese may believe that he himself is inherently as good as, perhaps, some of his friends and relatives, but he is not willing to concede these virtues to a stranger, especially a foreigner."

Risk-Taking Propensity

A universal fear of being charged with not upholding the national interests of the PRC greatly inhibits risk taking.

One major outcome of the Cultural Revolution was the development of a cautious attitude within the Chinese in general. This is known as "the disease of lingering fear." Unless a Chinese negotiator is certain how an initiative will be received, the best course is to do nothing. This reluctance to take risks and the need to be sure before acting contributes to meticulous, astute, and tough negotiators who can negotiate for long periods of time.

Internal Decision-Making Systems

While Chinese rhetoric points to a participative decision-making style, numerous third-order controls result in an authoritarian system.

In traditional China, the individual did not make his own decisions. With so much life confined to, and controlled by the family, adjustment to the established group and to its opinion was the supreme requirement.

While there is participation in the decision-making process, the premises of such decisions are governed by numerous third-order controls. These controls range from managerially imposed limits on information to cultural and political norms of correct action. So, the decision-making process becomes a ritual of participation with no real decision-making power. Of course, such a

Form of Satisfactory Agreement

Chinese decision makers are well aware of the advantages of avoiding precise written commitments as to their part of the agreement and of including precise commitments for the foreigner.

Zhang Zhinfu, Chinese Minister of Finance, said, "Our friends can rest assured about the protection of rights and interests of foreign partners in economic cooperation. We Chinese always mean what we say and live up to our words." And it is true that the Chinese always stress the importance of honoring international contracts.

The Chinese are strict constructionists in their approach, and their goal is to arrive at carefully worded contracts. The Chinese appreciation of the significance of written reports and legalistic documentation includes the realization that they can be protected when something is not included in the written contract. The objective of the Chinese is to avoid precise written commitments for themselves and to receive precise written commitments from foreigners.

Holding Chinese partners to agreements, written or otherwise, is more difficult than it might seem. The Chinese are not troubled by suddenly cancelling contracts. These terminations, while extremely disturbing to foreign businesspersons, are consistent with cancellation clauses included in the contract. But even without the cancellation clauses, it is likely that, should circumstances change, the Chinese will not hesitate to cancel agreements.

Concluding Scenario
Do Foreigners Have a "Chinaman's Chance" in China?

The Chinese seem to follow a Frank Sinatra train of thought in that they wish to look back on their business interactions with foreigners and sing, "I did it my way." It follows that one who does business with China must be willing to do it on Chinese terms. Given the nature of Chinese terms, this demand is unacceptable; however, it is also untrue and can be discarded as a bluff if the foreign investor has something the PRC wants.

There will be problems for Americans and other foreigners, though, in convincing the Chinese that their stand is unwavering.

however, it is also untrue and can be discarded as a bluff if the foreign investor has something the PRC wants.

There will be problems for Americans and other foreigners, though, in convincing the Chinese that their stand is unwavering. Too many U.S. and foreign corporations, including some major oil companies and banks, have given in to Chinese demands.

Given the possibility that foreign corporations may achieve a satisfactory agreement, one must still question the wisdom of major investments based on potential long-term gain. This is especially true for the 1990s or until the old men die and new stable leadership and policies emerge. Consider the following:

1. There are no contractual guarantees in the PRC that supersede political variables.
2. The circumstances of the PRC are changing. The biggest problem is the foreign trade deficit, which is soaring. There is also a decline in grain harvests. Of the $16 billion in pledges of foreign investment since 1979, little has gone where the government needed it most, i.e., into high technology, transportation, and energy.
3. The change in Chinese circumstances is already resulting in major disappointments. Up to this point, according to Landy Eng, president of the Asian Business League in San Francisco, for every ten companies entering the PRC, nine have returned with big holes in their pockets.

In the short term, foreign businesspersons should require contract terms that allow immediate gains, either in countertrade or specific amounts of foreign exchange, keeping in mind that guaranteed returns are never guaranteed.

References and Suggested Readings

1. Bonavia, D. *The Chinese.* New York: Lippincott, 1980.
2. Chu, Chin-ning. *The Chinese Mind Game.* Beaverton, OR: AMC Publishing, 1988.
3. DePauw, John W. *U.S.-Chinese Trade Negotiations.* Praeger, 1981.
4. Hall, Edward T. *Beyond Culture.* Garden City, N.Y.: Anchor Press, 1981.

5. Hinton, H.C. (ed.). *The People's Republic of China: A Handbook.* Boulder, CO: Westview, 1980.
6. Hsu, F. *Clan, Caste, and Club.* Princeton: D. Van Nostrand Company, Inc., 1960.
7. Kapp, Robert A. (ed.). *Communicating With China.* Chicago: Intercultural Press, 1983.
8. La Barre, Weston. "Some Observations on Character Structure in the Orient: The Chinese," *Psychiatry,* November, 1946.
9. Oxname, Robert B. and Richard C. Bush (eds.). *China Briefing.* Boulder, CO: Westview Press, 1981.
10. Pye, Lucian. *Chinese Commercial Negotiating Style.* Cambridge: Oelgeschlager, Gunn & Hain Publishers, Inc., 1983.
11. Pye, Lucian W. *Asian Power and Politics.* Cambridge, MA: Harvard University Press, 1985.
12. Szuprowicz, Bohdan and Maria. *Doing Business With the People's Republic of China: Industries and Markets.* New York: John Wiley & Sons, 1978.
13. Zeigler, Harmon. *Pluralism, Corporatism and Confucianism.* Philadelphia: Temple University Press, 1988.

10
·········
NEGOTIATING IN SOUTH KOREA

Introduction

Korea has accomplished much over the past decade. The country of the Great Han People has grown economically from a poor third-world country to a highly industrialized nation. The standard of living has substantially increased and democratic movements are continuing.

In September 1988, Korea hosted the XXIV Olympic Games. For the first time since the 1976 Montreal Games, athletes from communist and non-communist blocs met in Seoul, enhancing the true Olympic spirit and making the Seoul Olympics the most successful ever in terms of global participation. The fact that Korea hosted the Olympics exemplifies the great strides that Korea, a country once thought to be backward and undeveloped, has made in global economic circles. Rising above a tumultuous past, Korea has shown that a commitment to internationalization, plus a hardworking and industrious people, has broken solid and long-standing political barriers and obstacles. As its trade volume increased, the exchange of officials, scholars, athletes and tourists to many countries particularly the United

States has also increased. Culturally, as well as economically, Korea slowly but surely joined the global game. Korea is indeed at the threshold of a new and exciting era as it has established itself as an economic model for the developing nations of the world.

Historical Perspective

Since 1945, Korea has been divided into a northern zone called the People's Democratic Republic of Korea and a southern zone called the Republic of Korea (South Korea).

South Korea covers 38,211 square miles, or about 45 percent of the Korean peninsula. The population is estimated at over 42 million. Seoul, the bustling capital city, is located in the northwest corner. Pusan, on the southeast coast, is a special city headed by a mayor who is directly responsible to the central government.

The legend of Tangun relates that in the twenty-fourth century B.C., the son of the Creator turned a bear into a woman and mated with her, producing an offspring named Tangun who descended on Kangwha, a large island off the coast of Inchon, and became the ancestor of all the Korean people.

Modern archaeological findings indicate that the earliest Korean peoples were migrants and invaders from present-day Manchuria, Northern China, and Mongolia some time before the eleventh century B.C.

Throughout much of the 2,200 years of their recorded history, the Korean people have found themselves between powers greater than themselves, and the Japanese colonial rule over Korea from 1910 to 1945 is often remembered with bitterness by Koreans.

After World War II, America opened its doors to Asians, and Korean immigration gradually increased. Korean laborers were first employed in the United States to work on the Hawaiian sugar plantations. At the turn of the twentieth century, Korean immigration quickly decreased. Although the Korean community is one of the largest and fastest-growing groups among the four main Asiatic groups in the United States, Americans, in general, know little about Korea. Koreans, in fact, established themselves on the six continents, a major feat considerating Korea's long and tumultuous past.

From 1910 to 1945, the Japanese occupied Korea as a result of the Russo-Japanese War. The Japanese first dominated, and then completely absorbed every facet of Korean life, from banks, to religion, to industry and agriculture. With the coming of World War II, Korea was turned into an arsenal factory for the Japanese war effort. However, even with the Japanese surrender in 1945, Korea was denied her status as a unified nation. Korea was divided at the 38th parallel into two trusteeships, the northern half under the Soviet Union, the southern half under the United States. The U.S. trusteeship lasted until the constitutional First Korean Republic was founded in Southern Korea in 1948. However in 1950, North Korea invaded the Republic of Korea, starting the Korean War. It was at this time that most Americans discovered Korea, searching the world atlas to find out where President Truman was going to send U.S. troops. Three years later an armistice was signed, separating North and South Korea by a demilitarized zone.

Since the uneasy peace began over thirty years ago, the Republic of Korea has made giant strides to overcome the disadvantages of being separated from its northern half, which had a stronger industrial base. In three decades of hard work, which was at times interrupted by political unrest, the Republic of Korea built itself into an industrial power that for its size rivals its neighbors, Japan, Taiwan, Hong Kong, and Singapore.

Much of the country's strength comes from the Korean people themselves, a hearty, hard-living people who have retained their cultural identity even after centuries of imposed political, social, and economic changes. Korea values education for its children above all things. The Korean literacy rate is above 90 percent, and a strong education is the main source of the competitive global spirit businesspersons have come to expect from their Korean counterparts.

Korea now stands at the threshold of a new order in international relations. It has demonstrated its economic strength by expanding markets and improving the growth and quality of its products. The images of political repression in Korea have begun to fade, as Korean diplomatic competence and global sensitivity have expanded. If Korea continues along these paths with the zeal it has shown in recent decades, its international position will be further strengthened.

The Twelve Negotiating Variables

Basic Concept of the Negotiation Process

Paramount to the Korean culture is the need to maintain harmony. One of the main concepts of Confucianism is the search for harmony in all that one does. This concept of harmony comes from the chief virtues of filial piety, a combination of loyalty and reverence that demands a son show respect to his father and fulfill the demands of his elders. Ancestor veneration, in which members of the family must not breach etiquette or perform any act that would bring disrespect or discredit upon their ancestors, stems from this belief.

In negotiations, establishing the right *kibun* is of critical importance. *Kibun* is the dominant factor influencing conduct and relationships with others. The word literally means "inner feelings." If one's *kibun* is good, one functions smoothly and with ease. If one's *kibun* is upset or bad, things may come to a complete halt. The word has no true English equivalent, but "mood" is close. In interpersonal relationships, keeping the *kibun* in good order often takes precedence over all other considerations.

In negotiations, Koreans operate in a manner that will enhance the *kibun* of both persons. To damage the *kibun* may effectively cut off relationships and create an enemy. Indeed, one does not do business with a person who has damaged one's *kibun*.

Selection of Negotiators

The Korean negotiating team is selected on the basis of status, knowledge, and expertise.

Respect for elders, the family, education and people in power are paramount to the Korean culture. To engender the anger of an elder means serious damage because his age allows him to influence the opinions of others, regardless of the rights or wrongs of the situation. In the presence of an elder, one remains at attention, not even smoking or drinking. Like children, elders must be given special delicacies at meals, and their every wish and desire is catered to whenever possible.

But Korea is changing and its leadership is becoming more of a bimodal industrial elite. This group consists of members in their fifties and sixties and individuals in their thirties. In the past, the elders were regarded as the decision makers, but now one is just as apt to find a younger individual involved in the decision-making process. These individuals are competent, dedicated, highly educated, trained and often the descendants of founders. Those with a high education are more respected. Most large corporations feature an individual as a figurehead who will be the chairman. The president is normally the top executive power, with a vice-president or executive managing director next in line of importance.

Role of Individual Aspirations

In Korea, groups are traditionally more important than the individual, and the family and its relationships are the most important elements in society. The importance of the family is taught to children before they go to school and is fostered in the educational process. This ideal is reinforced in all aspects of Korean life.

These values carry into the business environment, and the idea persists that the group is the most important element. Maintaining harmony within this sphere is paramount.

The most successful and largest Korean companies foster an atmosphere of family, loyalty, and commitment among employees. Besides their other functions, supporting these ideals is one of the main responsibilities of senior management.

Concern with Protocol

General protocol and tenor of Korean business discussions are very important. Korea is a formal society.

The use of names in Korea has a different connotation than in most Western countries. To the Confucian, using a name is somewhat presumptuous and impolite, as a name is something to be honored and respected. In Shamanism, to write a name calls up the spirit world and is considered bad luck. A name, whether it is written or spoken, has its own mystique, and is regarded as personal property.

In Korea, there are relatively few surnames, thus there appears to most Westerners to be an inordinate number of Kims and Parks. A

Korean is addressed by his title, position, trade, profession, or some other honorific title such as teacher. As opposed to saying, "Good morning, Mr. Kim," a polite "Good morning" is better. Many Koreans work and live next to each other for years without even knowing their full names. The president of South Korea is referred to by high officials as "Excellency," even in his absence, because it is considered too familiar to use such a high person's name in conversation. A Korean's name is usually made up of three characters—the family's surname is placed first, and then the given name, which is made up of two characters.

Physical contact in business, other than a handshake, should be avoided; it is considered outright disrespectful. Physical space is a private domain and should be observed. Korean women present at an office or a reception should be acknowledged with a slight nod, not a handshake.

The presentation of a business card is most important, and should take place before the beginning of any discussion. It is considered an extension of the individual presenting it, thus, it should be offered with dignity. The right hand should be used for the presentation. Cards should include the visitor's name and professional identification in his own language, and on the opposite side, the same information should be presented in Korean.

Formality in dress should also be observed. White, long-sleeved shirts are considered an indication of serious commercial endeavors. Ties should also always be worn.

Koreans who fail to observe the basic rules of social exchange are considered by other Koreans to be less than a person—he is a "nonperson."

All foreigners, to a certain extent, are considered by Koreans as nonpersons. Koreans show less concern for a nonperson's feelings or his comfort. However, every effort must be made to remain within the framework of polite relationships.

South Korea is a socially stratified society. The establishment of proper social and business relationships is of extreme importance to Koreans, and Confucian teachings have had a great impact on Korean attitudes and values. Rituals of courtesy are ever-present, and formality in behavior is the rule. Public modesty, when speaking of one's family or achievements, is the norm, and harmony with one's family, friends, and business colleagues is important.

Significance of Type of Issue

Relationship-based issues are very important to Koreans, but as with other Asians, Koreans are also concerned with other substantive issues.

Coming from the religious background of Confucianism, sincerity and good intentions of one's counterparts are significant. Initial introductions are highly valued, and Koreans prefer to deal with individuals who are respected by their peers. Koreans are gift givers, even at the first visit.

They are known to haggle over price. They will therefore automatically raise the opening price so that in the end, they may make a better deal.

Complexity of Language

The Koreans are considered high context communicators. Asian languages are on the extreme end of the high context grid. More often it is not what is said that is important, but what is not said. Though Koreans are becoming westernized in their approach in doing business and are exposed to lower context languages such as English, the underlying culture still requires that the foreigner be aware of the importance of nonverbal patterns.

Physical contact in business, other than a handshake, is considered disrespectful. Displays of emotions should also be avoided. Whether negative or positive, they reduce privacy and are best repressed.

Nature of Persuasive Argument

The need to maintain harmony is paramount. It is the Asian way to bargain, but in doing so, it is critical to maintain harmony and never openly criticize others in public. Saving face is a critical issue and should include any condition that might be perceived as humiliating. The avoidance of conflict and reconciliation are basic to the preservation of self-esteem. Harmony and modesty are a way of life, and all people are shown respect and approached with humility. Great care must be taken to avoid offense or harm to another.

Value of Time

Punctuality should be adhered to. One should arrive at all meetings on time. Because of other commitments, a Korean businessperson may sometimes keep a visitor waiting. This can occur as a result of time pressures on senior executives as well as the propensity to view a new engagement as less important than an ongoing event.

Lower-level managers are occasionally not quite as time sensitive as might be expected. Because planning and execution are administered from the top down, a waiting posture is assumed in hopes that clarification and direction will emanate from higher executive levels.

Bases of Trust

Trust develops slowly and through past experiences. Koreans form relationships with foreigners slowly and subtlely. They prefer to deal with individuals they know well or who have been recommended by friends or other business associates. Once a relationship has been developed, it will continue through years of business.

Risk-Taking Propensity

Koreans avoid risk because of their desire to maintain face and harmony. Care must be taken in all circumstances to ensure that actions or words are not taken or misconstrued as criticism. To embarrass someone by making a joke at his expense is highly resented, even if it is done by a foreigner who does not understand the customs.

Internal Decision-Making Systems

Business and social lives are tied to groups and group structure. The Confucian ideology continues to have a deep imprint on business decision making. Equality and participation are school subjects, not management principles. Paternalism and autocracy are ingrained. Major transactions will inevitably require either approval by, or at least consultation with, planning bodies or concerned ministries. Group stability is desirable and the formal functioning of the group is the optimal operating method with loyalty at the core. Most decisions will be made at top levels, where frequently the senior person still rules by inspiration and through charisma.

Form of Satisfactory Agreement

All contracts with Koreans will and should be formalized in writing. At times, Koreans have a propensity to leave several clauses flexible so that should the need arise during the effect of the contract, changes can be made. It is best that all critical issues be in writing and that extensive notes be taken during the actual negotiations to clarify issues if necessary later.

Concluding Scenario
A More Stable Korea

There is still considerable unrest in Korea. Strikes, wage-increase demands, as well as student movements demanding more democracy, make the government somewhat uneasy. However, many believe the new Democratic Liberal Party, by cleverly balancing the rival factions, may rule for many years.

A great number of foreign investment projects in Korea have been authorized in recent years. Principal investors are by rank Japan, United States, Hong Kong, Britain, West Germany, and Saudi Arabia. Major areas of investment have been in the hotel and tourism industry and in manufacturing and mining.

South Korean construction companies have also developed internationally recognized construction and engineering techniques. Under the Five-Year Development Plan, they have undertaken huge projects, including construction of dams, highways, tunnels, and factories. Construction orders have increased both domestically and abroad.

To sell in Korea, it is useful to have the assistance of a Korean registered agent. All registered agents (there are over 2,000 such firms) belong to the Korean Traders Association (KTA). The "Exalted 13" are Korea's 13 General Trading Companies (GTC) and are powerful within the Korean economy.

During the past three decades the Republic of Korea has grown tremendously in economic areas, mainly through hard work, careful planning, and close identification of individual and business interests with the economic goals of the nation. For the United States and other countries to be successful in business ventures with the Koreans, these Korean interests and goals must be respected and incorporated into the foreign companies' business policies.

Korea's sixth Five-Year Economic and Social Development Plan (1987-1991) is under way. It calls for diversification, export expansion, and more expenditures on social services. A changeover from direct government control to an economy run by market forces seems to be occurring within the country. Exports will increase as Koreans become more interested in exporting sophisticated and technical goods to other parts of the world.

On the political scene, the January 1990 merger of the governing Democratic Justice Party and the opposition Reunification Democratic Party resulted in a two-party political structure. On the right is the Democratic Liberal Party led by Roh Tae Woo, and on the left is the Peace and Democracy Party led by Kim Dae Jung. The merger and the resulting political strength of President Roh is expected to help control the occurrence of illegal strikes and significant wage increases that hurt Korea's ability to compete in the world economy.

South Korea has much to offer foreign markets, including good entrepreneurial skills and an educated and disciplined labor force.

The future holds great promise for mutually beneficial trade relations between Korea and the United States. Foreign businesspeople should learn more about North Korea as the two countries will undoubtedly be reunited.

Korea, the Land of Morning Calm, has been transformed in just thirty years from an impoverished agricultural country into an industrial state that is quickly approaching advanced status in global business. Korea holds great promise for the future as it is close to becoming one of the world's top ten trading nations. The strong economic surge of Korea seems to have gained a tremendous momentum, one which foreign business persons would be negligent to ignore.

References and Suggested Readings

1. Barnett, Angela. *Korea: How to Understand Our Relationship With Korea.* Sacramento, CA: The American Intercultural Consultation Group, 1988.
2. Bunge, Frederica, M. (ed.). *South Korea, A Country Study*, 3rd ed. Washington, D.C.: United States Government, 1982.
3. Chun, Karl (ed.). *Korean Annual 1986*, 23rd ed., copyright 1986, Yonhap News Agency.
4. Covell, Jon C. *Korea's Colorful Heritage.* Si-sa-yong-o-sa, 1986.
5. De Mente, Boye. *Korean Etiquette & Ethics in Business: A Penetrating Analysis of the Morals and Values That Shape the Korean Business Personality.* Chicago, IL: NTC Business Books, 1989.
6. *Koreans: Building Bridges of Understanding.* Provo, UT: Language Research Center, Brigham Young University, 1976.
7. Mitchell, Tony. *Simple Etiquette in Korea.* Norbury Publications, Ltd., 1985.
8. Morse, Ronald A. (ed.). *Wild Asters: Explorations in Korean Thought, Culture & Society.* Woodrow Wilson International Center, U. Press of America, 1987.
9. Schmidt, Klaus. *Doing Business in Korea.* San Francisco State University, 1980.
10. Steinberg, David I. *South Korea Profile.* (Profiles-Nations of Contemporary Asia Ser.), Westview, 1986.

11
....

NEGOTIATING IN INDIA

Introduction

India, the world's second most populous nation, is a country of sharp contrasts. Tradition coexists with modernity, and mud hovels stand beside elegant high-rises and luxury hotels. Although farmers produce bumper crops, thousand of Indians still starve each year. India is often perceived as a land of abject poverty, where children beg in the streets alongside mysterious snake charmers. Cows, an animal sacred to the Indian people, are thought to roam freely through villages and major cities. But in reality the world's most populous democracy is becoming a leading industrial and military power. Not long ago, India's restrictive investment policies gave foreign firms little reason to consider the Indian market. These policies are changing as Indian officials recognize the importance of acquiring technology and capital goods from abroad for the modernization of India's industrial sector. Liberalization of India began under Prime Minister Indira Gandhi. Today India is one of the ten most industrialized countries in the world, providing growth markets and offering opportunities for foreign investors in the 1990s.

During the reign of Rajiv Gandhi, regulations were lifted on many industries, and simplified industrial licensing for small and medium-sized companies became possible. This new business climate in India, emphasizing building modern capital-intensive industries and investing large resources in high technology, is providing American, European, and Japanese firms major opportunities to invest in high-technology sectors, particularly electronics, telecommunications, computers, and power plants. Under Prime Minister, Mr. V.P. Singh, the focus is on agriculture and rural development.

The combination of new and old worlds in India presents various problems for the foreign businessperson wanting to invest or establish a subsidiary in India.

Historical Perspective

The people of India have had a continuous civilization since 2500 B.C., when the inhabitants of the Indus River Valley developed an urban culture based on commerce.

In the tenth and eleventh centuries, Turks and Afghans invaded India and established sultanates in Delhi. In the early sixteenth century, descendants of Genghis Khan entered India and established the Mughal (Mogul) Dynasty, which lasted for 200 years.

The first British outpost in South Asia was established in 1619 at Surat on the northwestern coast of India. In the late 1600s, the East India Company opened permanent trading stations at Madras, Bombay, and Calcutta. The British gradually expanded their influence until, by the 1850s, they controlled almost the entire area of present-day India, Pakistan, and Bangladesh. British rule lasted until 1947 with Britain directly administering most of India, allowing few selected areas to be governed by local rulers with direct supervision.

In the early 1920s Mahatma Gandhi instigated a massive movement against the British colonial rule that resulted in independence for India on August 15, 1947. Longstanding frictions between the Hindus and Muslims led the British to create two countries out of British India—India became the homeland for Hindus, and Pakistan, the homeland for the Muslims.

After receiving its independence, India had a succession of Prime Ministers, one of the most notable being Indira Gandhi who ruled from 1966 to 1977 and returned to office once again in 1980.

Mrs. Gandhi is credited with starting India on the road to liberalization and economic reforms. Following her assassination in 1984, her son assumed the position of Prime Minister, initiating new programs as well as altering existing government regulations in an attempt to attract foreign investment and business. Rajiv Gandhi left office in late 1989 when he was defeated in the national elections by Mr. V.P. Singh.

India, about one-third the size of the United States, has a population of over 800 million people, second only to China, with 15 percent of its people under the age of fifteen. With an annual population growth rate of over 2 percent, it is estimated that India will surpass China by about the year 2012 to become the most populous country in the world. Like China, India spreads through many geographical and climatic regions, but is most varied in the complexity of her peoples and languages. Sixteen officially recognized languages are spoken in India.

The complexity of India and the relations between the different peoples are complicated by a unique Indian caste system. In spite of elaborate promises in the constitution about equality, caste is still a reality.

Indians are fatalists, believing that life is predestined. Theoretically a person cannot break out of his caste in his lifetime; he has to wait for reincarnation and hope that he has merited rebirth in a higher caste. There are four main castes: Brahmin (priests), Kshatriya (warriors), Vaishyas (merchants or traders), and Sudras (lowly or menial).

In its foreign relations, India tries to protect its power advantage over its neighbors and prevent outside intrusion and, at the same time, actively seeks foreign financing, technology, and arms trade. While India has a solid relationship with the USSR, which is a strongly valued source of economic and military supplies, India is moving to broaden its diplomatic relations, particularly with the United States, to achieve greater access to the U.S. markets. It has also strengthened its relations with western Europe to diversify its source for arms and gain further access to the high-tech trade market.

The Indian people are religious, family-oriented and philosophical, believing strongly in simple material comforts. Because of their fatalistic attitude towards life, most Indians are content with their lot, believing that nothing is by accident in the universe. This outlook makes them highly elastic and therefore open to compromise in situations necessitating negotiation. Being a humble people, they do not look favorably on those who display conceit or who are overly self-confident. They conduct business under relaxed, relatively formal conditions, preferring low-key presentations to high-pressure tactics. The concept of social harmony is very important in the Indian way of life. This attitude carries over into their business relations. They emphasize the importance of establishing a good rapport between the two negotiating partners before engaging in the business at hand.

The Twelve Negotiating Variables

Basic Concept of the Negotiation Process

As negotiators, Indians are a resilient people who are more than willing to compromise to obtain what they want. The British influence is evident in their reserved, formal conduct; therefore, the tone of negotiations should be serious and subdued. Correct manners in India are governed by the rule that behavior should conform to the social situation. A sure failure in conducting negotiations with an Indian businessperson is to act cold or aloof. The Indian tone is humble and modest, and negotiations should be conducted without high-pressure tactics or the display of conceit or high-handedness on the part of the foreign negotiating team.

The Indian businessman is similar to his Chinese counterpart in that both emphasize building relationships and establishing a rapport between the two negotiating parties.

Indians view negotiations as a truthful way of solving problems mutually. The focus is to find a solution that will please everyone involved. *Satyagraha,* a Hindi term that means "firmness in a good cause," is the way Gandhi approached negotiations.

The concept of "facilitation payments" or bribery is an accepted and common practice in the Indian business environment; therefore, foreign companies entering the Indian market must be prepared to deal with this situation if it arises in the negotiation proceedings. Having "connections" is important. Nepotism is strong, and each layer of society has its own "old boy network." The visitor without an introduction is an unknown. If at all possible, a negotiator should have a liaison, such as a politician, lawyer, or professional in the country, who can perform the necessary introductions.

Selection of Negotiators

Selecting a negotiating team in India is complicated because the status differences among the members must always be considered. Indians put much importance on maintaining social harmony, and it is imperative that the negotiating team be able to work together as a group.

Top management does not view lower ranks with confidence; therefore, they have not been trained to function independently. All decisions are made from a higher management level. Indian managers have a paternalistic attitude toward their subordinates and thereby feel that delegation of power and responsibility would unfairly and unduly burden lower level employees.

The Indian negotiating team consists of the technicians who possess expertise in a certain area as well as representatives of the company management.

Role of Individual Aspirations

Individual members of the team do not attempt to stand-out among their colleagues, and Indian management is based on the personal touch of the individual. Group functioning, committee work and consensus decision making have been generally unsuccessful because of the differences in the status of the individuals.

An important factor for the Indian worker is security on the job. In a society where unemployment increases daily, it is imperative that the Indian laborer feels secure and confident in his position. Most Indians are satisfied to do their job and leave all responsibility and decision making to higher management.

This centralization of power has direct bearing on the negotiation proceedings. All decisions are made from the top; therefore, the decision process is quite slow and drawn out, a practice fairly uncommon to the American businessperson. To speed up the decision process and make certain that their proposals have been understood, the foreigner should leave a positive impression at the decision-making level. By using intermediaries and bestowing certain small tokens of appreciation on various individuals, the foreign businessperson can ensure the continued flow in the negotiation process and may obtain quicker results.

Concern with Protocol

Experienced Indian negotiators have found Indians to be patient, amiable, and understanding. They are known to be tolerant and accepting of those who are unfamiliar with their customs and beliefs but are also impressed by those who attempt to adapt to the Indian way of life while in their country. Although the negotiations follow formal procedural outline, the atmosphere will be friendly and relaxed. The Indian team members will always be polite, expecting the same courtesy from their counterparts.

In following the British tradition, using titles to convey respect is an important part of Indian society. When dealing with Indian businessmen, it is proper to address important Indian executives by their last name only or by their title, for example "Mr. Chairman." A common form of address a subordinate may use for his manager is "manager Sahib," but this is not appropriate for foreigners.

Visitors to India should observe certain simple procedures. Indians, as a people, are sensitive and easily slighted. Foreigners who display general ignorance of local affairs are perceived as looking down on India. Visitors must also be careful not to look down upon or talk down to one's host. They should not enter, sit, or smoke without invitation, and it's imperative to avoid using the left hand when greeting someone or eating food because it is considered the unclean hand.

Significance of Type of Issue

Indians consider relationship-based issues most important. The Indians put great stock in building relationships with their foreign counterparts. This emphasis on establishing a working rapport between sides before actually entering into the formal negotiating process can be time consuming, and Americans find negotiating with India a fairly long and involved process.

Negotiators must also be concerned with the substantive issues of relative price, reliability, after-sale service and most importantly credit. Labor savings as well as long-run efficiency is of less concern to the Indian businessman because of the availability of manual labor. Local service, both marketing and technical, is essential, requiring the existence of service facilities on Indian soil. In price negotiation, bargaining is an accepted practice, but only small margins need be incorporated into the initial offering price.

Complexity of Language

In personal and business relations, Americans use direct and honest speech and criticize those who have a tendency to beat around the bush. Indians also are concerned with honesty and trust in a relationship, but they believe that maintaining social harmony is an important factor in business relations. Therefore, it is not uncommon for an Indian negotiator to answer a question according to what he thinks the other party would like to hear. By accommodating the foreign team, the Indians are not lying or trying to be ambiguous, rather they wish to maintain harmony and a good working atmosphere. This tendency leads many Americans to accuse the Indian businessman of deliberately stalling for time in order to gain an advantage over their opponents.

Nature of Persuasive Argument

Because many Indians are fatalists, believing in predestination of one's life, they are most likely to use either empirically-based reason or ideology as an argumentative style. All events are controlled in the universe, and Indians, although open to compromise, are likely to state the facts or conditions of a situation and conclude that this is how things are and, therefore, must be taken at face value. Being a subdued and mild-mannered people, Indians do not like public displays of emotion. They conduct themselves with maturity and wisdom and value self control over impulse. This reserve is an important factor in initiating good business relations, and

Indians do not condone emotional outbursts, attributing such displays to lack of maturity and self control.

Value of Time

The American concept of time is how much can be accomplished in the shortest possible period. Today's Indian executive understands the importance of time and even judges others by their punctuality, but he is also aware of the effectiveness of letting others deliberate their Karma (fate) while sitting in the waiting room. Because Indians emphasize relationships between potential business associates, negotiating in India can become complex and somewhat more time consuming than the normal American businessperson is accustomed to.

In negotiating with an Indian, two elements are essential, namely (1) the foreigner's ability to exhibit extreme patience and (2) education. A thorough explanation of the situation, such as why a deadline is critical, is vital to success.

Bases of Trust

Trust must be earned. Before the Indian bestows the gift of trust on an individual, he/she must first develop a relationship with that person to decide whether he is worthy of that trust. Conveying trust is also important in the negotiating process. The foreign team must understand and accept the Indian's need to establish relationships before actually entering into negotiations. By demonstrating patience and willingness to allow the Indians to set the lead, the foreign team will make a positive impression on their opponents, which in turn can lead to a favorable outcome.

Risk-Taking Propensity

The Indian businessman is a humble, low-key individual who is conservative and fairly formal in nature. Because most Indians are fatalists, believing that one's destiny is determined before birth, they are willing to accept things for what they are, without question. This attitude towards life allows them to be open to compromise and to take certain risks because the resolution of the situation has already been decided.

Internal Decision-Making Systems

The Indian business environment continues to be centralized with little responsibility delegated to non-management levels. Although the Indian negotiating team will have representatives from various departments, decisions will be made by top management. This practice has worked well over the years and continues to be accepted by employees and managers. This procedure may prove a hindrance in the negotiations because foreign delegates will rarely have direct contact with top management and will not have the opportunity to personally defend their position.

Form of Satisfactory Agreement

Following Anglo-Saxon tradition, a handshake in India is a signal that an agreement has been reached and that business has been concluded. Naturally all agreements should be committed to paper, and an official contract should be drawn up. Indian law follows British precedents and contracts are settled in court under provisions of the commercial code and common law. In this system, oral evidence not incorporated in written documents may become important testimony in future legal action, so it is imperative to include all detailed stipulations of the agreement in the contract to prevent any possible complications in future business relationship.

Concluding Scenario
Will India be a New Market of the '90s?

India is one of the world's most exciting growth markets and offers opportunities for foreign investors in the 1990s. A nation experiencing strong social and economic change, India is ripe for domestic and foreign investment.

Indo-U.S. commercial relations have deep roots. U.S. presence is seen in many aspects of the Indian economy, as the United States is one of India's major trading partners and a major collaborator in joint-venture and technical agreements. This year Citibank celebrates its 86th year in India, the only country in Asia where the bank has operated continuously since its opening.

Until the late 1970s, commercial relations grew gradually. In addition to India being half a world away, various restrictions on the private sector and Indian government policies protecting domestic industry caused most U.S. businesses to view India as a difficult market to break into. High tariff barriers and import licensing restrictions excluded a wide range of U.S. exports, and foreign investment was subject to severe restraints. Yet even under these circumstances, many American companies entered the Indian market, and now, with the numerous changes being implemented by the government, India offers a myriad of advantages to those looking into foreign investment, acquisition of a local business, or the establishment of a foreign subsidiary in the country.

The following are important positive factors:

- With an annual population growth rate of 2 percent, India is poised to overtake China by the early twenty-first century as the world's most populous nation.
- Although one of the oldest existing democracies in the world, the Indian government continues to keep tight reign on the business community. The government owns and runs various public enterprises such as the railways, power facilities, and the airlines. Since becoming independent in 1947, successive governments have emphasized national self-reliance, which continues to be the motto for Indian planning.
- India has the world's fourth largest military machine, after the United States, Soviet Union, and China, and the government is planning to develop advanced-weapons systems locally as well as building the Indian Navy into the undisputed leader of the region.
- The use of English is common in the Indian business world making it less complicated for American firms to conduct business in the country.
- India, in addition to Bangladesh, Bhutan, Maldives, Nepal, Pakistan, and Sri Lanka, is a member of the South Asian Association for Regional Cooperation (SAARC). This organization, established in 1985, encourages cooperation in agriculture, rural development, science and technology, culture, health, and population control. This association could open new markets for foreign companies and allow for a greater diversification of sales.

- India now has the world's third largest pool of scientific manpower and continues to produce scientists, engineers, and doctors at a rate that by far outstrips its economy's capacity to absorb them.

In spite of the current commercial and economic reforms taking place in India as well as the concentrated efforts of the government and local businesses to attract foreign investors, one cannot ignore certain negative features evident in the Indian business environment.

- An estimated 288 million Indians, about 36 percent of the population, live below the poverty line. The issues of homelessness and food distribution are urgent, and the vast differ- ences between the rich and poor have caused much unrest in India.
- The extensive caste system may also be a disadvantage to the foreign business looking to establish operations in India. Social restrictions placed on an individual because of his caste cannot be ignored.
- Although the Indian government has eased off considerably on commercial restrictions concerning foreign and domestic business ventures, the Indian market is still much more complex and difficult to enter than some other international environments. Overseas investors' perception of India's investment climate is mixed.
- National strikes and employee walk-outs, although less of a problem than in other industrial nations, are still a common occurrence in India and may cause certain hardships for the foreign firm's operations.
- India's foreign debt is a matter for great concern. The problem facing the government is the runaway spending triggered by economic liberalization. The country's foreign debt has climbed 65 percent in four years and foreign exchange reserves have dropped so low as to cover barely two and one-half months of imports.

After considering the positive and negative aspects of the Indian business environment, the question remains if India will become the new market of the 90s. Although India's business environment is not an easy one in which to operate, the country's size and economic potential add up to a profitable market for those who understand the challenges of the system and develop the skills to work within it.

References and Suggested Readings

1. Chellaney, Brahma. "Passage to Power." *World Monitor*, February, 1990, p. 24–32.
2. "India." *Asia-Pacific Forecasting Service*, 1989.
3. *India Background Notes*, March 1988. Political Risk Services. Frost & Sullivan, p. A1–A7.
4. *India Culturgram*. Provo, UT: Brigham Young University Publication Services, 1988.
5. Moore, Clark B. *India, Yesterday and Today*. New York: Bantam Books, 1970.
6. Roy, G.C. *Indian Culture*. New Delhi, India: Ajanta Publications, 1976.
7. Schmidt, Klaus D. *Doing Business in India*. Business Intelligence Program, p. 10–23, 1979.
8. Sweeney, Leo. *Republic of India*. Kansas City, MO, 1970.
9. The Statesman Year Book 1986/1987. New York: St. Martin's Press, 1986, 123rd ed.

12

·········

NEGOTIATING IN THE USSR

Introduction

To most businesspersons trained in the West, the Soviet Union represents a complex and mysterious environment. As a socialist country that rejects free enterprise, the Soviet Union nonetheless engages in trade with capitalist countries and is rapidly changing its views on free enterprise. Such trade is forcing an integration of the two systems and mandating certain changes in attitude and preconceptions.

Since 1917 when the czars lost control, all power is centralized in and controlled by the Communist party. Every major post in the country is occupied by a party member. Membership is, however, restricted. Only six percent of the population belongs to the party. It is obvious that a small elite group holds the reigns of power.

The party's Central Committee and the Council of Ministers are responsible for the majority of the decisions in the USSR. The Five-Year Plan is the driving force behind the country. The Plan, rather than market forces, is used to determine the supply of goods and to solve the economic problems. The decisions that are made at the top are then passed down to the lowest levels. Obviously, the Soviet system offers few lessons in the area of compromise. There is little give and take in the policy-making process, but Mikhail Gorbachev almost single-handedly is changing this.

Historical Perspective

The Union of Soviet Socialist Republics is the largest country in the world, measuring 8.65 million square miles and stretching across eleven time zones. This vastness is protected on every border, except for the Polish frontier, by natural barriers. This, in addition to a long history of foreign invasion and Russia's early affiliation with the Orthodox Church, has led to a sense of isolation and a general mistrust of foreigners—especially Westerners.

More than 100 nationalities live in the Soviet Union. Although Russian is the official language, over 130 languages are spoken within this country. The largest ethnic group is the Eastern Slavs who account for 70 percent of the population. Other groups include the Turks, Baltics, Mongolians, and Eskimos.

Besides the variety of ethnic groups, the Soviet Union contains many religious groups. The State, however, strictly regulates religious expression. It regards religion, which Karl Marx called "the opium of the People," as unnecessary. The State alleges that 70 percent of its population is atheist.

During World War II, Joseph Stalin attempted to unify his country around the concept of "Mother Russia." This emphasis continues today as Soviet leaders try to reshape nationalistic ethnic groups into loyal supporters of the USSR.

The Soviet Union is divided into 15 republics that, according to the Constitution, are sovereign states. In fact, Moscow retains control over the entire system. The largest and most important union republic is the Russian Soviet Federated Socialist Republic. It accounts for 75 percent of the land mass and over 50 percent of the population.

The USSR is also an intriguing country because of its diversified historic, economic and political evolvement. An historical perspective is necessary to comprehend the effects of the current reforms introduced by Gorbachev. Russia has always been a powerful country, although it has never reached its economic and technological potential. During the seventeenth and eighteenth century, czars encouraged Western European influence on the Russian culture, but resisted market forces or any sign of modernization. Even though Russia's industrial take off was difficult, by 1914 it became the world's fourth most powerful industrial nation. It was unrealistically powerful because even though its per capita output was high, its national product was exceedingly low.

After the Bolshevik Revolution and World War I, Russia's economy was in ruins. Under Lenin's militaristic power, the Russian economy became centrally organized with production targets fitted to the framework of a development plan. Russia's economy was strengthened by developing oil, steel, and textile industries. By 1945, Russia led East European economic and military groups including The Council for Mutual Economic Assistance (CMEA) and The Warsaw Pact.

Russia's political and economic system was rigorously based on Marxist principles until Mikhail Gorbachev took power in 1985. During the late 1980s reforms were designed to decentralize control and restructure the Russian economy. *Glasnost* was one of the major reformations. It relaxed state control over cultural, intellectual, and religious activities, and opened official state activities to public scrutiny. *Perestroika* was another major reform aimed at decentralizing government authority and promoting a degree of democracy.

These reforms have had profound effects on management techniques and trade. Some major national companies are now allowed a certain degree of autonomy to improve production facilities and to develop an incentive system based upon quality and quantity of production. These reforms have also had a positive impact on international business. Soviet citizens are now encouraged to form cooperative enterprises and to enter into joint ventures with Western organizations. The Soviet government hopes to double the volume of foreign trade by the year 2000 by enabling companies to engage in foreign trade.

US/USSR political and economic relations have improved since the "Gorbachev Revolution" started, but the cold war period is too recent to accurately assess this new era of reformation. To most Americans, the Soviet Union is still a strange and remote land.

Winston Churchill's description of the USSR remains real: a riddle wrapped in a mystery inside an enigma.

US/USSR trade has not significantly increased over the last few years even though Soviet foreign economic policy aims at improving bilateral trade relations. Only one percent of U.S. trade takes place with the Soviet Union, and U.S. exports to USSR account for only two billion dollars of mostly agricultural goods. The Soviet Union is the world leader in petroleum production, coal mining, iron ore, mineral fertilizer, cement and steel, but it has a one trillion dollars demand for scarce, unavailable consumer goods as well as a need for industrial modernization.

The Twelve Negotiating Variables

Basic Concept of Negotiation Process

Historically, negotiation is seen as a competitive process in which the Soviets seek to maximize their gains at the other side's loss. Using distributive bargaining, they seek a "zero sum" result whereby they win. The Soviet system offers few examples of compromise (the word "compromise" in Russian has been borrowed from another language). The Russian negotiator is tough and shrewd and makes concessions cautiously.

Soviets also use the negotiating process as a part of an overall effort to secure national interests.

Soviet negotiations have traditionally involved political issues but, at present, business negotiations with foreigners are increasing because of the new reforms. As a result of the new reforms, power has been slowly delegated and control is becoming increasingly decentralized. Russians now have more freedom to make their own decisions in business negotiations, but they still are unfamiliar with foreign procedures since most have been isolated from Western culture and politics for many years. According to tradition, foreign business negotiations take place through the state, and their decision-making process is oligarchical. All business transactions, including overseas trade, are conducted through the Ministry of Foreign Trade. Foreign negotiators must accept the Soviet bureaucracy that is involved in the decision-making process for all proposed projects.

Soviets have been known to be great power negotiators. They can be confrontational, blunt, and combative negotiators. Although most state negotiations are conducted with a power approach, commercial negotiations are now more likely to be conducted on a win-win basis. In forming joint ventures, participants often develop strong personal loyalties, and a give and take between the American and Soviet partner often emerges. Soviets generally conduct business with a sense of decency and humanity, but the negotiation process can be very slow. Soviet officials are attentive to decorum and to protocol, and alternate formal sessions with social periods that feature food and hospitality. Companies that conduct business according to Russian guidelines display great patience. However, once a company is established, business activity is usually stable. The success of these ventures comes from the fact that competition is slow and marketing techniques of local enterprises are inefficient.

Selection of Negotiators

The Soviet negotiator is a professional and is selected on the basis of his ability, experience, and specialization. Soviet negotiating teams have a great deal of continuity; the members of the team work together for many years and become a cohesive unit. The Soviets often complain that when they deal with Western delegations, the faces are never the same.

Since *perestroika* was introduced in 1987, Russia has had a need for Western expertise. Policy makers want to learn Western business concepts, including marketing and advertisement, and are eager to learn about management skills. Russians want to learn how Western businesses work and how to trade in the U.S. market. Several American management consulting firms have already entered the Soviet market.

Russia's progress has been limited by its backward technology. Soviets want to attract top-quality specialists who can help modernize the old-fashioned techniques used by local organizations. They give high priority to joint ventures that demand industrial modernization.

Soviet management qualifications differ from those in the West. The system is limited in that there may be many highly qualified specialists (engineers, architects, etc.), but no generalists. The USSR has no business schools. Westerners going into the Soviet Union are providing their expertise and are even being asked to establish business schools.

Role of Individual Aspirations

In the past individual aspirations have played a limited role in the Soviet Union. The Communist government advocates serving the people, thus emphasis on the community is strong. Subjected to strong pressure from the top, the Soviet negotiator's personal aspirations remain suppressed.

The decision-making process is also centralized; therefore, people cannot decide what they would like to do. Communism has limited individual aspirations. However, these traditional socialist ideals are changing and more individual freedom is allowed. Soviets can now engage more freely in commercial negotiations and possibly realize their individual goals.

Concern with Protocol

The Soviets show strong concern for the setting of negotiations and are conscious of protocol. A negotiator should be aware of the various tactics they might employ to manipulate the environment to their advantage. They might conduct long sessions at times and places convenient only to themselves or unpleasant to the opponent. This practice is often used in commercial negotiations. Another tactic is the control of the agenda, since the negotiation is conducted in their own country.

When commercial negotiations are initiated, they tend to be dominated by low-to-mid level specialists who are not permanent members of the negotiation team. These sessions tend to be relaxed, with everyone contributing opinions and questions, but the mood changes at later stages. Discipline and hierarchy become important since Soviets are sensitive about age, rank, and protocol. In the interest of maintaining negotiations, Americans should show the appropriate levels of respect.

Traditionally, Soviets enjoy ceremony and certain formalities, including speeches and dinners. At present, Soviets who deal with U.S. companies in joint ventures are mostly interested in results. The Soviets, like Americans, now believe time means money.

Rules for self-presentation are formal in Russia. These rules should be followed to create a good first-hand impression and prevent irritations. Russians should always be addressed by their complete names. They usually use their first name, plus the patronymic, and finally their surname. This procedure can be confusing to Americans because of the complexity of the language, but remembering the complete name in the correct order is of utmost importance.

Since the reforms were introduced, interests in clothing have changed. The Soviets are buying designer wear from the French, Italians, Scandinavians, and Americans. The stereotype of the Soviet woman in a large, gray overcoat and babushka is an image from the past. At present, women have a strong interest in fashion and cosmetics and various other products on the new import list.

Significance of Type of Issue

Substantive issues dominant state negotiations. Russians are said to be hard bargainers and use premeditated tactics to achieve their best alternative. Personal relationships have little significance when it comes to bottom-line decisions. Commercial negotiations, on the other hand, give more attention to procedural issues. Since the late 1980s, these negotiations have been conducted on a personal basis. They involve an interest in personal and mutual gain.

For the Soviets, price and terms are main concerns. When a Soviet begins the negotiation, he has already been supplied with clear objectives and a range of concessions, and, he is concerned with meeting these outlines.

Complexity of Language

In the USSR there are more than 130 spoken languages and five different alphabets with one mother tongue base—the Russian language. Even though the Russian language is based on a different alphabet, cyrillic, and is difficult to understand, Americans can relate to the context of the Russian language and culture. The Russian culture and language are of low complexity. Their pattern of communication stresses the significance of verbal cues rather than non-verbal ones.

Nature of Persuasive Argument

In the initial stage of a US/USSR negotiation, Russians show little interest in order to exhaust Americans and yield their concessions. Soviet negotiators know that Americans feel frustration and failure when agreements are not reached. They take advantage of this American attitude and delay negotiations. Soviets show interest in a negotiation by walking away and just saying "No."

Value of Time

Negotiation periods are often long, arduous and demanding because of the Soviet bureaucracy involved. Actual negotiating time on a project will usually range from a few weeks to a few months for sales, and from one to several years on licensing arrangements and more complicated sales. Negotiators must deal with the Ministry of Foreign Trade, representatives from the industrial ministries, and sometimes business leaders. Each of these three groups have different objectives, and agreements are not easily reached.

Soviets may also use time to delay negotiations in order to yield concessions from the Americans. Their logic is based on two Soviet assumptions about American business people. The first is that Americans regard compromise as both desirable and inevitable, and the second is that Americans feel frustration and failure when agreements are not reached promptly. The Soviet's delaying strategy is not always successful, but it is always present in the Soviet consciousness and is impossible to avoid.

Bases of Trust

It is important to understand the nature of the Russian system before trust can develop. Russia has a centrally planned bureaucratic system that differs from the American capitalist system. Because of the many reforms currently taking place, the Russian system is unpredictable and may be risky for foreign investors. It is difficult to trust a system of this nature, though the effects of the changes may seem attractive to foreign investors.

Trust may vary depending on the sector with which one negotiates. Most commercial negotiations belong to the market sector. This sector has some degree of decentralization in its decision-making process and its management. Negotiations conducted through this sector may be easier to trust because much of the bureaucratic dealings have been minimized. These negotiations are usually conducted on a personal basis and strong personal loyalties usually develop.

State negotiations are part of the planned sector and are conducted with a hard bargaining power approach. One should use caution in trusting these negotiations because the Russian participants are primarily interested in maximizing their own interest at the expense of others.

Risk-Taking Propensity

Russians are cautious in making decisions because they prefer avoiding uncertainty. Since the Soviet system is centrally planned, there is no incentive to accept a risky negotiation even though it may generate higher returns. Eyes are not focused on a corporate bottom line, so the Soviet Foreign Trade Organization may not be interested in quickly concluding profitable business proposals.

Russians prepare preliminary analysis of proposals to evaluate risk. Before commercial trade negotiations begin, the Soviets prepare a comprehensive forecast plan. The plan usually contains clearly stated Soviet goals and anticipated U.S. responses to various Soviet moves.

Internal Decision-Making Systems

In negotiating and obtaining approval for a joint venture, the Western partner must lobby extensively with various Soviet agencies. The process begins with acquiring support from the senior official within the Industrial Ministry. If the minister is not personally involved, negotiations may not be approved. The Western partner must also make certain that other Soviet ministries and organizations agree to conditions or provisions involved in the negotiating process. Under the joint venture, the Soviet partner is responsible for obtaining these approvals.

Before the Industrial Ministry and the Republican Councils of Ministers formally approve the joint venture, various ministries review charter documents and the feasibility study. The Ministry of Finance reviews the financial viability of the venture and its impact on hard currency earnings, and Justice reviews the documents to assure conformation with Soviet law. Finally, the Foreign Trade reviews the pricing of goods and services sold on the domestic market and the impact of the joint venture's overseas sales on the existing trade activity.

Form of Satisfactory Agreement

In general, Russians are good at creating clever contracts. These are generally wordy, ambiguous, and omit important details so that they can be exploited to the Soviet advantage at a later date.

For commercial negotiations, the Foreign Trade Organization (FTO) offers one of its own form contracts and urges its adaptation. Most FTO's have several variations of their purchase form contracts, each suitable for a different type of transaction. The forms may range from a simple two-page agreement to a complex agreement that may include additional licensing.

Concluding Scenario
Perestroika, Glasnost and ?

Business leaders often ask, "Are *perestroika* and *glasnost* really working, and what changes have resulted in the Russian negotiator's approach to negotiations?" Most analysts agree the question is difficult to answer. The Soviet Union provides a market with extraordinary opportunities for investors, but because of the changes currently taking place, its market is unpredictable and transitional. Gorbachev introduced *glasnost* and *perestroika* to decentralize control and restructure the Russian economy. The effects of these reforms are not clear, but they seem promising to American business people.

The Soviet management system has been greatly affected by the reforms. The New Enterprise Law has had profound effects on business practices, as it provides some degree of autonomy for major national enterprises. Management decentralization has also impacted the 15 Soviet republics. Each republic now has the authority to engage directly in foreign trade and make decisions regarding the transaction. The results should yield more aggressive and energetic republics with new opportunities for trade.

Even though these changes might have promising effects in the long run, at present much potential political instability exists in the Soviet Union. A new venture carries with it an extra measure of risk, but the USSR represents a significant and untapped market for American businessmen.

References and Suggested Readings

1. Berliner, Joseph et al. *Assessment of Managers.* New York: Free Press, 1979.
2. Davies, R.W. *Soviet History in the Gorbachev Revolution.* Billing and Sons, Ltd., 1989.
3. De Pauw, John W. *Soviet-American Trade Negotiations.* New York: Praeger Publishers, 1979.
4. "Doing Business with the Soviet Union." *AMA Management Briefing.* AMA Membership Publication Division, 1988.
5. Knight, Misha G. *How To Do Business With Russians.* Greenwood Press, Inc., 1987.
6. Scherer, John Z. *USSR Facts and Figures Annual.* Academic International Press, 1986.
7. Shukman, Ann. *The Semiotics of Russian Culture.* Michigan Slavic Contributions, 1984.
8. Sloss, Leon and Scott Davis. *National Negotiation Styles.* Department of State Publication, 1987.
9. Smith, Hedrick. *Doing Business With the Russians.* Praeger Publishers, 1979.

13

....

NEGOTIATING IN GERMANY

Introduction

In 1989 dramatic changes occurred in West and East Germany. The Berlin Wall, which stood since August 1961 as a physical reminder of the more than forty-year division of Germany into two separate countries, came down. Almost totally destroyed after World War II, free-market oriented West Germany, also known as the Federal Republic of Germany (FRG), managed to evolve as one of Europe's most powerful economies. East Germany, or the German Democratic Republic (GDR), belonged to the Eastern Bloc countries with a centrally planned economy. East Germany, as one of the Soviet Union's satellite states, became a member of COMECON (Eastern Bloc trading organization) in 1950. West Germany was one of the driving forces towards the Western European Community (EC) since the early 50s. The two countries united in October 1990.

West Germany, in contrast to East Germany, never officially accepted the division into the two Germanies. Its constitution even contained provisions outlining their reunification. Now, dramatic changes, unquestionably influenced by Gorbachev's continual shift in politics towards the West, have taken place. After months under dual pressure of unceasing flight to the West, and continuing demonstrations, East Germany opened its borders with the West on November 9, 1989—a historic event.

Today, a reunited Germany is a reality. Whether this one Germany will be integrated into NATO as a whole, or whether it will resume neutrality, is hard to predict. At this stage, however, it seems almost certain that the German question can only be solved within the broader framework of the European theater.

Germany's internal reorganization will have an immense impact on the rest of the world and might inevitably affect the world's economic and military power balance. Against this background, it will become even more important for Americans to successfully negotiate with their German counterparts.

Historical Perspective

Germany's history is long. The area that is now called Germany has gone through many changes. The most significant of these was the eventual unification of the many Germanies.

Starting with the Thirty Years' War from 1618 to 1648, which was concluded by the Peace of Westphalia, the German government was completely fragmented. Prussian dominance, implemented by a professional army and civil service, emerged in the eighteenth century under King Frederick II the Great, of the Hohenzollern princes of Brandenburg, whose capital was at Berlin. After a disastrous loss to the French at Jena in 1806, Prussia helped defeat Napoleon at Leipzig in 1813 and at Waterloo in 1815. The division of Europe directed by the Congress of Vienna in 1815 increased German territory and set up the German Confederation, a loose union of 39 independent states. By 1834, most of these states were also members of the Zollverein, or "customs union." The continent-wide revolution of 1848-49 involved uprisings by impoverished German farmers and workers and the founding of the first parliamentary government in Germany. Austria was excluded from Germany as a result of its defeat by Prussia in the Seven Weeks' War of 1866. The following year, Chancellor Otto von Bismark brought together the German states north of the Main River in the Prussian dominated

North German confederation, and after defeating France in the Franco-German War 1870-71, he founded a united German Empire under William I of the House of Hohenzollern. Under the militaristic policy of William II, Germany supported Austria against Russia and launched World War I (1914-18). The German defeat cost the country, through the Treaty of Versailles of 1919, its overseas colonies as well as European territory and huge reparations. The Weimar Republic that ruled from 1919 to 1933 was beset by economic depression and was succeeded by the Nazi (National Socialist German Workers' Party) dictatorship under the infamous Adolf Hitler. With Hitler in control, the German war machine awoke once more and invaded Poland on September 1, 1939, which launched World War II.

After total defeat of the Germans, the Americans spent an incredible amount of money for the reconstruction of Western Europe. From 1948 to 1952, the Marshall Plan helped restore industrial and agricultural production above prewar levels. The economic miracle resulted in the emergence of West Germany as one of Europe's economic powers. With its free-market oriented philosophy, West Germany became interested in American methods of doing business.

Today West Germany is an economic world leader, trailing only the United States in total exports. Its ever growing economy makes it one of the most influential countries in the world.

The Twelve Negotiating Variables

Basic Concept of the Negotiation Process

German negotiations are planned and well organized. Conflict is seen as dysfunctional and a symptom of being unprepared. It wastes time that could be used for more useful discussion. Germans are direct in their approach to negotiations and are usually well prepared. Discussion is likely to be precise and direct. Negotiators are interested in getting right to the hard facts. Business relationships are also competitive. Germans view the negotiation process as a way to further the interests of the company/government as a whole.

Selection of Negotiators

Over 40 percent of all German managers have an engineering-related education. Another 20 percent come from the field of theoretical economics. Most of these managers have been trained in the fundamentals of industrial administration as a foundation of scientific business management.

Negotiators are predominately men. Women only make up about nine percent of management despite outnumbering men in the total population.

Experience is extremely important. In Germany, a man at age 35 is said to be getting ready to take responsibility. A man in his mid-50s is said to be in his prime.

Negotiators are typically selected for their knowledge of the subject to be discussed. Knowledge of the facts is important because emphasis will be directed toward the discussion of facts and details.

Role of Individual Aspirations

The Germans are generally team oriented. Their goals are to further the interests of the company or government. However, there is also an element of *wichtig tun*, or *"acting important."* When a visitor attempts to make an appointment with an executive, the secretary is likely to automatically direct the request to lower levels, even though the executive is available. This is a serious game on the part of German executives. They take any opportunity they can to confirm a gained or imagined position.

Concern with Protocol

German protocol is formal. Germans are conservative in dress and expect their counterparts to be conservative as well. They believe seriousness of purpose goes hand in hand with serious dress. Anything that is flashy and too fashionable is best avoided. Germans see correct posture as a sign of inner discipline.

Prescribed manners are of utmost importance. Business meetings are traditionally started with a handshake of all parties involved. This is followed by the offering of a seat by the German hosts.

Germans consider themselves to be polite and expect visitors to recognize this.

The visitor should use pleasantries such as *danke* (thanks) and *bitte* (please) liberally. He should also be aware of the protocol of the left and right side. For instance, when a junior executive is walking with his senior manager, the junior executive usually walks on the left side, the side of deference. With a woman, the man should walk and sit to her left.

When passing through a doorway, the senior manager or visitor passes first. At times, however, this turns into a game of, "no thanks, after you." In this case, or when in doubt, the visitor should pass first.

Titles are important. They are used liberally to develop respect. Some titles are:

Geschaftsfuhrer—top man
Generaldirektor—general manager
Direktor—top level manager
Abteilungsleiter—department head

Significance of Type of Issue

During negotiations, Germans tend to keep a distance between themselves and their negotiating counterparts, as they feel the development of personal relationships might interfere with the negotiating process. Formality is highly respected, and is thought to create an efficient atmosphere for negotiations.

Negotiators will spend most of the time concentrating on the facts and details of the proposal, and substantive issues are predominant.

The Germans will also spend time with procedural aspects. They look for a well planned, well organized negotiation that will be efficient and effective, and they use agenda setting and organizing as a means of achieving these goals.

Complexity of Language

The German language is low context and Germans use low context communications. Non-verbal cues and signals are not widely used in Germany. Eye contact is important, but is consistent, hence not used as a cue.

The Germans do not appreciate emotional gestures. Hands should be used with "calculated dignity," and never used as lively instruments to emphasize points in conversation. The goal is to appear calm under pressure.

Nature of Persuasive Argument

The Germans are definitely skewed toward empirically based reasoning, and knowledge of all the facts and details is essential. Negotiators should use brochures, samples, technical data and any other means to illustrate the thoroughness of their preparation and the quality of the products. Germans appreciate precise factual presentations. Numbers that support statements should be used liberally to illustrate points, since this is what the Germans will be using in their presentations.

Value of Time

Time is essential. Germany is without a doubt a monochronic society. The visitor should be sure that he is on time to all appointments. Germans are punctual and expect the same in return. If the visitor is punctual, he probably will not wait long before being admitted to the meeting.

Bases of Trust

The Germans shy away from using their intuition in trusting their negotiating counterparts. They concentrate on the past performance of the individual or company. Trust is not as important in Germany as it is in most other countries, yet once trust has been lost, it is difficult to regain. Contracts for the most part are written. These written agreements will be precise and will leave little room for ambiguity or interpretation.

Risk-Taking Propensity

Germans are considered low risk takers. Their risk avoidance can be understood in light of their history. During the world depression of the late 1920s and early 1930s, Germany faced inflation so intense that stores had to close every few hours just to raise prices. Since that time, Germans have become rather conservative in their approach to business situations. This risk avoidance, however, should not be confused with a lack of innovative business practices.

Internal Decision-Making Systems

The decision-making process flows from the top down through the organization. Decentralization of decision making is widely discussed, yet it is rarely practiced.

German society is paternalistic in nature. The father is the head of the household, and a boss-as-father relationship also carries over into the workplace. Under code termination, labor enjoys a voice in decision making, yet paternalism in Germany has yet to be seriously challenged. Because of the German fascination with facts, information represents power, and power is the basis for decision making.

Decisions will not be made until the negotiators have had time to thoroughly digest the facts.

Form of Satisfactory Agreement

The German side may give a verbal signal that an agreement has been reached. It is more common, however, to have a time lag for the Germans to digest the related facts and come to a final decision. In this case, a written document will constitute evidence of the agreement.

All agreements will ultimately be executed in writing. The Germans are explicit in their form of agreement. German agreements are in effect, "nailed down;" no room is left for interpretation.

Concluding Scenario
Germany's Warriors of Negotiation

In some respects, Germans and Americans seem to be alike. They are time conscious and want to get things done. Because most Germans are eager to speak English, the American will usually enjoy the advantage of negotiating in his own language. The use of interpreters is rare. In spite of this familiarity, there are certain values within the German society that a successful American negotiator should understand. Germans are detail-oriented and precise. They want to really be sure that something will work before they get further involved. Therefore, they need time to carefully study the pros and cons of a particular project. They prefer to put their resources in a well thought through venture, rather than taking the American "give it a chance" approach. Along these lines, they usually are less short-term oriented than their American counterparts. Furthermore, Germans want to know where they stand, and take reliability almost for granted: if you say something, you better do it, otherwise your business relationship might be at stake. Germans emphasize top quality; the reputable "made in Germany" label is no coincidence.

Germans expect a successful businessman to have a sound educational background and to be well-rounded. A certain interest in politics might also be crucial and rewarding in a lasting business relationship. Self-made men are rare in Germany, for success in business is often related to a certain social upbringing. Americans dealing with Germans tend to underestimate the importance of socially adequate behavior, including manners. Before entering into an important business relationship, Germans prefer to carefully screen their potential business partners to determine whether they will live up to their standards.

Americans might find that it is easier to deal with one German at a time, rather than giving a presentation to an entire group. Germans are rarely enthusiastic about supporting a new idea. They tend to come up with possible negative implications (risk-avoidance), and group dynamics can prove of little help to the innovator in such situations.

Post-war Germany has always been an export-oriented economy. As a result, Germans are accustomed to business interactions with foreigners, and their traditional trade surplus seems to prove their success in this field. In the '80s, more than half of their exports were directed towards other European Community members, while about 10 percent went to the United States. In return, their U.S. imports accounted for about 6 percent of their total imports. Americans face a major challenge of maintaining or even increasing their exports to Germany. Therefore, successful negotiation skills are becoming even more important.

The intra-German focus on reunification might also affect German business relationships towards the rest of the world. The opening of East Germany, its privatization of business, and its need for money might result in promising business opportunities for foreign investors.

Doing business with East Germans, who over the last forty years internalized the mechanism of a centrally planned economy, will require an enormous sensitivity from American negotiators. At this point, nobody can predict whether the exodus of East Germans to the West, about 330,000 in 1989, and an estimated 600,000 in 1990, will continue. The draining of human resources, whatever the dimension might be, is not only contra-productive to the advancement of East Germany's economy, but also puts the elaborate West German social security system under pressure. The intended monetary and economic union of West and East Germany will undoubtedly have immense repercussions on Germany's economy and on its short-term and long-term approach to doing business with foreigners.

References and Suggested Readings

1. Ardagh, John. *Germany and the Germans: An anatomy of Society Today.* New York: Harper and Row, 1987.
2. Burmeister, Irmgard. *These Strange German Ways.* 14th Ed., Hamburg: Atlantick-Brucke, 1980.
3. Hall, Edward T. and Mildred Reed Hall. *Understanding Cultural Differences.* Yarmouth, Maine: Intercultural Press, Inc. 1989.
4. Owen, Smith E. *The West German Economy.* New York: St. Martin's Press, 1983.
5. Raiss, Lutz. *A History of Modern Germany.* Vol. 3, 1986.
6. Romer, Karl (ed.). *Facts About Germany.* Gutersloh: Lexikothek, 1980.
7. Turner, Henry Ashby. *The Two Germanies Since 1945.* New Haven: Yale University Press, 1987.

14

....

NEGOTIATING IN FRANCE

Introduction

France, the largest country in Western Europe, in many ways, symbolizes the essence of Western Civilization.

As a leader in literature, art, fashion, refined cuisine, and diplomacy, the French place significant emphasis on culture.

As people, "The French constitute the most brilliant and the most dangerous nation in Europe, and the best qualified in turn to become an object of admiration, hatred, pity or terror, but never of indifference," Alexis de Toqueville said. The French and the Americans have been bound in a long love-hate relationship. Politically and economically they have always had close ties, even though these ties were put to the test more than once.

French self-images stand out as a factor in negotiation. When "dealing with the French, behave like the French," is good advice for foreign negotiators.

In negotiations, the French follow their own logic, often referred to as "Cartesian" logic. The basic idea is that reasoning begins with what is known and then continues from point to point until a conclusion is reached. Thus logic is based on previously established principles. This devotion to principle might present some frustration for those negotiating with the French.

As a people, the French are proud, and this pride sometimes has been construed as an attitude of supremacy. They are a rationally minded people who regard individual accomplishments with the utmost respect and seem to care little of what others think of them. They march to their own drummer.

Historical Perspective

France was one of the first countries in history to progress from feudalism to the nation-state. Historically, astute ministers advised its monarchies, and its armies were the most disciplined and skilled in their day. During the reign of Louis XIV from 1643 to 1715, France was a preeminent European power. The French have continued to preserve their historical heritage and carry on their aristocratic traditions. Although writers portray France as leaning toward a more modern, pragmatic style of business, cultural values rooted in history prevail. As an international leader in the construction of nuclear power plants and the largest agricultural producer in the Common Market, the French have proved their expertise in world markets. French has existed as an international language since the early Middle Ages and functions as one of the official languages at the United Nations.

The mixture of amity and enmity that characterizes the relationship between France and the United States is partially rooted in the contrary development of the two nations. While the United States became a world power, France's international status declined. World War I brought great losses of troops and material and left France morally and economically exhausted. While struggling between the left and the right to find a new internal political direction, France increasingly relinquished its predominant role in the international arena.

When the Third Republic finally collapsed in 1940, it represented—despite the largest army in Europe—no serious obstacle to Germany's quest for continental supremacy. During the four years of occupation, France was split between the supporters of the Vichy regime of Marshall Philippe Pétain, who supported the German Third Reich, and de Gaulle, who tried to build up the resistance to ensure allied recognition.

After the liberation of France in 1944, de Gaulle led the first post-war government until the Fourth Republic was established under a new constitution with a parliamentary form of government. The Fourth Republic, like the Third, collapsed because of foreign policy problems dealing with Indo-China and Algeria. In 1958 a threatened *coup d'état* led the parliament to call again on General de Gaulle to become the first president of the Fifth Republic.

Gaullist diplomacy proved successful for nine years, until in 1968 students and workers took to the streets to express their dissatisfaction. Because of the chaotic economic situation and a political rebellion that threatened to get out of hand, President de Gaulle had no choice but to dissolve the National Assembly. The overwhelming majority voted for the Gaullists, frightened by a possible take-over by the communists.

In 1968, after a defeat in a governmental referendum, de Gaulle resigned, and George Pompidou became the new president. When Pompidou died in office in 1974, the fight for his succession split the Gaullist coalition, and Giscard d'Estaing became the first non-Gaullist president of the Fifth Republic.

The leftist parties achieved a historical success in May 1981, when Francois Mitterand defeated Giscard d'Estaing and was elected president. The first socialist government nationalized major industrial companies and banks. However, in 1982 it became obvious that the calculation did not work out. Company losses totaling $1.4 billion, declining exports, and increasing unemployment forced Mitterand to subsidize some companies in order to keep their competitiveness. However, the trade between France and the United States has proven to be quite stable and fruitful for both parties.

The Twelve Negotiating Variables

Basic Concept of Negotiation Process

Negotiation in France is treated as a logical problem. It includes careful preparation, research on possible precedents, and logically stated arguments leading to a solution. The French expect the other side to be prepared in the same way and to present logical counter-proposals. They love discussion and will even negotiate minor details. One common mistake foreigners make is to consider the negotiation as a series of discussions without clear purpose. That is not correct; discussions always have a purpose and are sometimes pushed to the extreme to study the other side's position.

The French also believe that conflict can be constructive and help progress. Their confrontations will be based on logical reasoning. Therefore, a concise, rational presentation of the pertinent facts is an effective counter tactic. Preparation is of key importance, for the French will leave no stone unturned. This combative nature often increases the overall time needed to complete negotiations. The French will not be pushed around. They expect direct and honest arguments and have a tendency to believe that win-win situations are the exception. They also expect the other side to have enough authority to make decisions at the negotiating table.

Selection of Negotiators

The French negotiating team is developed based on the status of an individual. Status includes the negotiator's social class, educational and family background, as well as his or her individual accomplishments. Social class is a key factor in that it often determines the schools one attends and the influence one's family enjoys. The way the French perceive the status of their counterparts will be an important influencing factor in the success of negotiators. Although women have achieved a significant presence in French business (40 percent of all French women have joined the workforce), they still have difficulty achieving similar status with their male equivalents.

Role of Individual Aspirations

The French respect individual accomplishments and focus on these as opposed to team accomplishments. It is important for the foreign negotiator to identify the correct individual to contact in the corporate hierarchy. Individual accomplishments have a large influence on status and control in the business community. The power and decision-making authority is highly centralized based in part on one's status.

Concern with Protocol

The French are extremely formal, and their attention to manners, courtesy, and respect is paramount in all business situations. Even interactions with personal friends in a business environment are kept extremely formal. This formality has implications for the foreign negotiator. The French can be expected to be courteous and respectful of any visitor; however, this should not be construed as the development of a personal friendship. Additionally, it is important to extend the same type of formality to the French. They are conservative in their body language, and although combative in their negotiating style, they are not accustomed to irrational outbursts. For best results, a foreign negotiator should initiate a meeting through a mutual and well-respected acquaintance of both negotiating parties. Discussion should be directed to the leader of the French negotiating team.

Significance of Type of Issue

Negotiable issues are more important than relationships, and French negotiators are primarily interested in identifying and analyzing the key issues of any negotiation. Developing a good personal relationship with their negotiating counterpart will most likely be minimal. The French tend to be guarded with their personal lives and relationships. They make a clear distinction between business acquaintances and personal friends. They are most interested in quickly getting down to business. The implication for the foreign negotiator is that initial "get-to-know-you" conversations will exist, but it will be limited and will most likely focus on talk of French culture. Gift giving is inappropriate. However, once a good business relationship is established, it will most likely be a long-term relationship.

Complexity of Language

The French use a mixture of high and low context communication in negotiations. Although their body language is conservative in comparison to other cultures, their negotiating style includes a lot of direct eye contact and their appreciation of debate indicates they value an accomplished style of rhetoric. However, the French are concerned with a concise, rational presentation of ideas in verbal and written form. All negotiations will be closed with detailed contracts preferably prepared in French.

Nature of Persuasive Argument

The French have a combative type of personality. They are receptive and appreciate a rational, factual, and logical presentation of issues in a direct and confrontational style. They approach the negotiation process through reason and methodically debate all issues. The foreign negotiator should be well-organized, factual, and rational in his or her presentation. The French are not receptive to hard sell techniques and may interpret such an approach as a method of distracting attention from negative factors. The best method dealing with the French is to give them all the facts, both positive and negative, and to rationalize the negatives away in terms of the benefits that will be realized.

Value of Time

The French are conscious of time in terms of their history and their accomplishments. The national emphasis on long-term economic planning carries over in business to long-term corporate goals and planning. Because of the division of these long-term goals, decision making is a slow process. Time is sometimes used as a negotiating tactic. The French expect punctuality, but will often keep a counterpart waiting as an initial demonstration of their control over the negotiations.

Bases of Trust

Trust is dependent on past performance and accomplishments. It is earned over time—not given at the beginning. Initially, trust is dependent on characteristics such as status, education, perceived decision-making authority, and association with mutual and trusted acquaintances. However, the attainment of long-term trust must be earned by one's performance. Because of the French feeling of superiority, it is often useless to try to impress. They are impressed by results.

Risk-Taking Propensity

The French are highly risk avoidant as is reflected in their confrontational style of argument and their focus on the primary issues of negotiation. Additionally, the general preference to have detailed contracts written in French and subject to French law indicates their need to feel fully protected in all contractual business dealings. Their whole orientation toward making rational, well analyzed decisions also reflects their need for security.

Internal Decision-Making Systems

Decision making in French corporations is highly centralized following the precedents of governmental decision making. Corporate structure places decision makers and decision making at the top levels of the corporate hierarchy. Identifying the decision makers during negotiation and directing the conversation toward them is extremely important. The same form of cooperative decision making which is found between all government levels and business at the national level can be found in the individual corporation among different hierarchical levels. However, the final decision will still be made at the top levels.

Form of Satisfactory Agreement

The French prefer detailed contractual agreements written in French. This is tied not only to their risk-avoidant nature, but is also a result of their attention to formality and their appreciation of the art of the written language.

Concluding Scenario

French history has been shaped by revolutions, wars, and conflicts. So too have French international business negotiations. To the French, negotiation is an art with long tradition in international diplomatic and business relations, with French negotiators and the French language at center stage. Therefore, a French negotiator is less interested in obvious bargaining—although he would not let a good chance pass by—than in searching out reasoned solutions for which he has carefully prepared.

Another important aspect in the art of negotiation is the French sense of formal hospitality and status. Supported by government or a company, a Frenchman sees his own role as one of prestige and authority. Therefore, a foreigner might sometimes have the feeling of inadequacy, which is not due to his own lack of ability, but rather to the high self-esteem displayed by his French counterpart.

However, once a foreigner has familiarized himself with the French *modus operandi*, and a relationship has been established, it will be, for the most part on a long-term basis; the French will prove to be compatible partners who may even warm up socially. When this happens, a foreigner will have the chance to experience the French people as friendly and humorous, and he/she will find that acceptance is based not on common achievements, but rather on personality. Personal character is rated highly among the French and respect has to be earned; it is not granted at the first meeting.

Another factor to be considered, particularly when dealing on a larger scale, is the simple fact that "French are first of all French." This holds true for companies as well as for the government, which will support any form of undertaking that is in the national interest while simultaneously finding ways to prevent any infringement of it.

The French motivation to work is different from any other nation's in the world. To the French, the only thing that really matters is the *qualité de la vie* — "the quality of life." The French work to live and do not live to work.

Past tensions with the United States have been reduced through the bilateral treaty of establishment (for each U.S. company seeking incorporation in France, a French company has to be allowed to incorporate in the United States). The French market will be open to European Community nations by 1992. This will require that companies be more competitive, and will likely force the French to be more accepting of foreigners.

France is ranked fifth among world economic powers. Its growth is resuming after a slowdown in the early 80s. As 1992 approaches, Mitterand and others believe a more powerful Europe will help France regain a more important role in global affairs. The French business community and banks jumped quickly on the 1992 bandwagon. But 1992 will bring both winners and losers to France, and only time will determine if past political and economic glories so missed will return to France.

References and Suggested Reading

1. Ardagh, John. *France in the 1980's: The Definitive Book.* Middlesex: Penguin Books, Ltd., 1982.
2. ———. *France in the 1980's.* New York: Penguin Press, 1983.
3. Barzini, Luigi. *The Europeans.* New York: Simon & Schuster, 1983.
4. Brinton, Crane. *The Americans and the French.* Cambridge, Massachusetts: Harvard University Press, 1968.
5. Carroll, Raymonde. *Cultural Misunderstandings—The French-American Experience.* The University of Chicago Press, 1988.
6. *Economist Business Traveller's Guides: France.* New York: Prentice Hall, 1988.
7. Hall, Edward T. and Mildred Reed Hall. *Understanding Cultural Differences.* Yarmouth, Maine: Intercultural Press, Inc., 1989.
8. House, John William. *France: An Applied Geography.* London: Methuen, 1978.
9. Peyrefitte, Alain. *The Trouble With France.* New York: Knopf, 1981.
10. Ross, George etal (eds.). *The Mitterrand Experiment: Continuity and Change in Modern France.* New York: Oxford University Press, 1987.
11. Schmidt, Klaus. *Doing Business in France.* San Francisco State University, 1980.
12. Schmidt, Klaus D. *Doing Business in France, Doing Business in India.* SDI International Business Program, 1978.
13. Wright, Gordon. *France in Modern Times: From the Enlightenment to the Present* (4th Ed.). New York: Norton, 1987.
14. Wylie, Laurence. *Village in the Vaucluse.* Cambridge, MA: Harvard University Press, 1972.
15. Zeldin, Theodore. *The French.* Vintage, 1983.

15

NEGOTIATING IN SPAIN

Introduction

Spain officially becomes a full member of the European Economic Community (EEC) in mid-1992 when its seven-year transition period comes to an end. Numerous changes have been occurring throughout the world, in Europe, and especially in Spain, in preparation for this event. *El Horizonte '92*—The Horizon of 1992—has become a powerful symbol of tomorrow's global horizon. Spain will also host several domestic events that will have tremendous international ramifications.

Barcelona, the capital of the Spanish province of Catalonia, has already begun to prepare for the 1992 Summer Olympics, with more than one billion dollars in improvements to the city, including the construction of new highways, subways, hotels, and an airport. The World's Fair, to be held in Seville, is expected to attract some twenty million visitors. The 500th anniversary of the discovery of "New Spain" by Christopher Columbus should bring large numbers of U.S., Latin American, and other foreign tourists into the country. Madrid has been selected by the EEC to be the "Cultural Capital of Europe" for 1992.

These outstanding happenings have spurred a number of educational, scientific, and cultural projects. Spaniards are ready and anxious to share not only their economic wealth but their cultural wealth with the rest of the world. The economic, cultural, and public-relations opportunities offered by the events of 1992 are obvious and the Spaniards intend to take full advantage of them.

Historical Perspective

The Spain of today is full of social, economic, and political changes that manifest themselves not only on the national level, but on a global level as well. Spain is being integrated into international spheres, especially with its acceptance into the EEC. It has begun a new epoch in its long and complicated history. Its renaissance is flourishing as Spain marches aggressively and anxiously towards the future.

Spain has reached an impressive stage of development in recent decades, and existing signals reinforce its continuing success. Spain, which was historically one of the greatest world empires, is once again on track towards an improved future. This time, however, Spain is not searching for riches in other parts of the world.

Spain has the potential for a brilliant future with the coming of 1992; however, it cannot look forward without taking note of its long and tumultuous history. The twentieth century has been difficult for the Spanish people. In less than a century, they lived through the reign and fall of a monarch, the establishment and fall of a republic, two dictatorships, and the return of the monarch in 1975. Forty of those nearly ninety years of political and social unrest and changes were during the regime of one man, Francisco Franco.

Franco became the leader of the Nationalist forces during Spain's bloody Civil War that erupted in 1936 with the uprising in Melilla of the African army against the Spanish Republican government. The Spanish Civil War became a major topic of international concern. Many countries aided the battling Spanish troops; however, this foreign aid only served to prolong the war. It was in April 1939 that Franco's Nationalists defeated the Spanish Republic beginning Franco's long and harsh rule as dictator.

Franco's dictatorship was severe in the area of the social, political, and economic freedoms of the country. He came to control almost every aspect of Spanish life, from language to literature, from production to exportation. After the Civil War, the objective of the agricultural and industrial politics was to assure a high level of self-sufficiency. The government control was harmful to the Spanish economy and industry, as it did not allow it to grow to the necessary level to compete internationally.

However in 1957, Spain finally started to move towards modernization. Franco's isolation came to an end and Spain opened itself up to the outside world. Tourists began to invade this balmy, mysterious land, and the tourism industry has grown continuously since then, making it today the main source of foreign exchange for Spain. With the advent of new ideas into the country, it was inevitable that changes would occur.

In November 1975, Francisco Franco died, leaving behind a country of 38.4 million people, a country slightly out of step, not quite modern, not quite backward. An extraordinary metamorphosis has taken place since Franco's death. One of the world's most enduring dictatorships has been replaced without violence by a progressive democracy with a king, Juan Carlos I, as constitutional head of state.

The new Spain that emerged is a different from the country that Franco ruled. Contemporary Western lifestyle is quickly replacing the traditional Spanish one. Spain underwent vast changes since joining the EEC, and its economy is now coming to the forefront as one of the most vigorous and innovative in Europe. The country actively accepts the challenge of converting into an increasingly important economic entity within contemporary Europe.

The Twelve Negotiating Variables

Basic Concept of the Negotiation Process

Spanish businesspersons view conflict as useful, and they attempt to solve stalemates directly, and with emotion, while stating their opinions. They use this technique in their *tertulias*, traditional intellectual meetings in which people discuss their different opinions.

Verbal responses are usually direct. Spaniards like to talk and to impose their ideas. Furthermore, they normally believe that what they say is much more interesting than what someone else says. As

Fernando Diaz-Plaja states in his book, *The Spaniard and the Seven Deadly Sins*, the proverb insisting that a dialogue is just a monologue with interpolations obviously originated in Spain.

Spanish pride is reflected in their negotiations. Both parties are allowed to present their views, but neither is convinced by the reasoning of his opponent. That is not to say that confrontation is inevitable in Spanish negotiations. On the contrary, direct confrontation should be avoided so that people do not lose face by having to admit an error. To accuse a Spaniard of being mistaken serves to infuriate rather than to correct him.

The predominant style of the business relationship is usually competitive. The Spanish will try to get as much out of the deal as they can. However, the visitor should take care to avoid any display of avarice. Everyone knows that the ultimate purpose of business is to make a profit, but no one talks about it. Towards the end of the negotiations, however, both parties are expected to get a fair deal. At this point, reciprocated expressions of trust are not uncommon.

Selection of Negotiators

Status is important and the Spanish upper class has power in politics, commerce, and industry. Therefore, belonging to an upper-class family or knowing someone with connections, can be of great help. In addition, knowing a member of these families usually means an introduction into the system. *Enchufismo*, that is, having the right connections, is crucial. Without these introductions, the foreign visitor will most likely have to languish in waiting rooms or converse with the powerless. A connection usually assumes an obligation in his introduction by assuring his Spanish counterpart that, "my friend is your friend." Such an assertion creates business pressure to perform as promised.

Usually the powerful are established in distinctive industries such as banking and law. The educational background of people is also important. The well connected usually attend one of the few private universities in the country or study abroad in Europe or the United States.

The sex of the individual is also a factor. Women are not powerful in Spanish business as few women occupy meaningful positions. This, of course, changes depending on the region and industrial sector. Catalonia, for example, has more women executives than

Madrid and for a woman to work in a bank is usually seen as prestigious.

The trend is changing with time. The highly structured social pattern is cracking. This means that promotion by merit and ability is increasing in Spanish business. Furthermore, the role of women in Spanish life is greatly changing. This trend can be seen in the large number of women now attending Spanish universities.

Role of Individual Aspirations

Individualism is ever present in Spain in all environments including business associations, church, and home. The Spaniard thinks he is special and unique. For that reason, every trait that he possesses is of inestimable value. As Havelock Ellis explains in his article, "The Genius of Spain," "the first characteristic of the Spaniard is his individualism. His contributions to the world have been the gifts of men who were mostly indifferent to the virtues of association and subordination, persons who were above all original, careless of their environment, daring to assert themselves."

El Viva Yo, or "my employer is very lucky to have me," is a common Spanish saying. Because a Spaniard regards himself as unique and special, a foreigner would be wise to compliment him often.

One of the most difficult things for the Spaniard to do is praise another. As Diaz-Plaja puts it, "the Spaniard can tolerate one or two admirable qualities in another Spaniard but never more. A man may be rich and noble, but not also intelligent and clever."

Despite his exaggerated individualism, the Spaniard is not isolated. In fact, one of his fundamental character traits is a sociability that at times opposes his individualism and at others feeds upon it.

Concern with Protocol

Everyone in Spain is concerned about protocol. In business circles, proper demeanor is important. The hallmarks of good manners are courtesy and style, and the Spanish negotiator expects his counterparts to behave the same way. However, the Spanish avoid being too formal or stiff. Such concepts would, in fact, be incompatible with Mediterranean extroversion.

Social class distinctions are important. One author suggests: "the visitor should not forget that strong barriers between social classes still exist in Spain. Therefore, the visitor should avoid fraternal gestures toward lower status employees."

Courteous and polite behavior is present in all aspects of negotiations, including the formal negotiations, lunch meetings, and even informal circumstances such as meetings in a bar or cafe.

Dress in Spain is formal and conservative. Dark suits and black shoes are essential for men. Businesswomen in Spain do not wear suits. Dresses and skirts are seen as more appropriate.

Significance of Type of Issue

Opening conversations usually center on nonbusiness issues. Spanish procedures require establishing personal rapport as a first step to building loyalty and trust. In the preliminary stage of negotiations, conversation centers on such topics as family and mutual friendships. Such topics as religion and politics are usually not part of a discussion. This part of the process can be time consuming, but can be as, or more important, than the "heart of the matter." The Spanish assume that once a friendship is established, the negotiating partner will feel obligated to give a preferential price.

As the negotiation progresses, tangible issues become more important. In this stage, substantive aspects prevail. The Spanish want to see samples, documents, and pamphlets. They also want to be given substantial information about the price and quality of goods. That is not to say that the personal-internal aspect fades away. As a matter of fact, meetings and conversation are quite commonly disrupted by trivial personal matters. When the personal problem is resolved, business matters can be resumed.

Complexity of Language

The Spanish use both verbal and nonverbal communication and rely on nonverbal language in everyday situations. Therefore, Spanish is a high context language.

The Spanish also place great emphasis on being articulate and clear in verbal communication. Because of their temperamental character, verbal communication is usually loud. At times a

Spaniard uses the same tone of voice for talking as a foreigner would use for disputing.

However, verbal communication is only a portion of the total communicative process. Nonverbal cues, such as gestures and facial expressions, are also used. Hands are as important as mouths when making a case. Eye movement is used constantly. A Spaniard with snapping eyes is either angry or impatient.

The use of the familiar *tu* form to the Spanish counterpart is usually a good sign. Physical contact is a sign of intimacy and friendship. When things go well, a Spaniard will often hold his counterpart's arm.

Nature of Persuasive Argument

The Spanish negotiator likes to talk. He likes to impose his values to convince his counterpart, but he does not readily accept his counterpart's opinion. When a Spaniard argues, he admits no points as superior to his own. Diaz-Plaja illustrates this point: "I remember a long controversy about how a word was spelled. At last, the one who was right launched the missile he had been keeping back for better effect. 'Don't argue anymore. That's what it says in the Academy's dictionary.' The other never blinked an eye. 'Then the Academy's dictionary is mistaken.'" This type of behavior is present in all circumstances, and business negotiation is no exception.

The Spanish negotiator uses skillful rhetoric with touches of emotion. His mode of arguing is similar to that of his French counterpart. The main difference is that, while the Frenchman uses rationality and logical reasoning in his arguments, the Spanish substitutes exaggeration. As Diaz-Plaja explains, "exaggeration serves the Spaniard's reasoning by multiplying the favorable evidence by a thousand and dividing the damaging testimony in the same proportion."

Value of Time

The Spanish view of time is polychronic, that is, time is plentiful. Spaniards treat time as if they own it, and they dispense it accordingly. This attitude prevails in all aspects of life. The stores, for example, are closed in the afternoon from 1:30 to 4:00. During this time people go home, eat slowly and if they have time, take a *siesta*. In addition, the Spanish take long vacations, from four to six weeks a year, and schools are closed from June to October.

The Spanish negotiator views time the same way. The foreign negotiator will most likely be kept waiting beyond a half hour. One can say that a prompt Spaniard is the exception rather than the rule. During the negotiations, progress will most likely be slow. Frequent interruptions, such as phone calls or a personal aside, are entirely normal.

A Business Intelligence Program Research Report describes the approach of the Spanish negotiator towards time: "The Spanish view negotiating as an enjoyable process; to them, results are almost by-products. Time for the Spanish negotiator is a frame in which developments occur; problems are best resolved after they have matured a bit. There is an implied assumption that everything will improve or resolve itself while time passes."

Bases of Trust

Negotiation usually requires a warming-up phase. In this stage, both parties establish personal rapport. Intuition and perceived status usually play a big role. This preliminary stage allows parties to know each other, and establish trust. Documented evidence and professional reputation are secondary.

If this is not the first time negotiations have taken place between both parties, past experience will be the determinant factor for building trust.

Risk-Taking Propensity

Spanish businessmen are usually conservative. They resist change until the last possible moment.

The Spanish negotiator, therefore, is mainly a risk avoider. His pride and individualism influence him to avoid image and power loss at all costs. The Spanish negotiator tends to choose a strategy that provides lower rewards but a higher probability of success.

In addition, the Spanish negotiator is intimidated by authority. He believes that there is an established hierarchy, and one cannot jump from one step to the other, but rather should act according to his role.

Internal Decision-Making Systems

Decision making is highly centralized. This centralist outlook can be traced back to the times of Isabella and Ferdinand or the times of Franco, who favored a tightly knit power structure as a means to obtain control.

Spanish businesses have a tight structure and people make decisions accordingly. Subordinates are conditioned to seek patronage from above; hence they often lack both training and practice in decision making. Their abilities are not highly valued. To ignore the chain of command means usually a serious reprimand, or even a loss of job.

Form of Satisfactory Agreement

An agreement is usually implicit and explicit. Similar to the contracts of most Latin American countries, Spanish contracts have implicit components. However, that is not sufficient. Spanish law and commercial codes leave little to interpretation. Therefore, a contract or an agreement is determined by its written content.

Concluding Scenario
El Horizonte '92

Historically, Spain has been relatively isolated from Europe, causing some scholars to remark that "Africa begins at the Pyrenees," which means: Spain is different from the rest of Europe. Life south of the Pyrenees does take on a distinctive flavor, one marked by bullfights, fiestas, siestas, and flamenco singing. However, Spain is no longer different; it is eminently European.

The English-speaking world had been fascinated by Spain for ages. Washington Irving spent much time strolling through Granada's Alhambra. Hemingway was enthralled by the bullfights and the many foreign volunteers who risked their lives in the Spanish Civil War. Spain casts a spell over her visitors, one that intrigues them and leaves them yearning to return, to see more, to know more. As James Michner says in *Iberia*, "philosophically the concept of Spain intrudes into the imagination, creating effects and raising questions unlike those evoked by other nations." Today the question most often raised is how to enter into the Spanish markets.

Spain's entrance into the EEC in 1986 was the culmination of a long economic modernization process. Many multinational corporations have already established themselves in Spain or are in the process of establishing manufacturing plants and distribution systems. Spain offers low wages, highly qualified workmanship, short training periods, the lack of labor disputes, and an attractive and extensive domestic market of more than forty million consumers.

Foreigners contemplating working in Spain should consider several factors. Negotiating styles are much less formal in Spain than in other countries, and it is customary to negotiate during lunch and dinner meetings. There is a social atmosphere surrounding business ventures. However, at the same time, the social hierarchy plays an important role in Spain's complex society. Spaniards use a network of personal relationships, *enchufe*—or "plug in," which is similar to networking in the United States.

Spain is divided into seventeen autonomous regions, each with its own culture and history. Spanish (or Castilian) is the official language of the country; however, the regions also have their own official languages. Of these, Catalan, Galician, and Basque are most predominant.

Opportunities certainly exist in Spain. Nearly 500 years ago, Spanish leaders financed commercial expeditions that transformed their country and the world. Today once again, Spain has the chance to influence global events and shape the future.

References and Suggested Readings

1. *Background Notes—Spain.* United States Department of State, Bureau of Public Affairs, December, 1987.
2. *Doing Business in Spain.* Price Waterhouse & Company, 1986.
3. Kompass Espana, SA, Kompass Espana. New York: IPC Business Press, Ltd.

4. Lieberman, Sima. *The Contemporary Spanish Economy: A Historical Perspective.* London; Boston: Allen and Unwin, 1982.
5. Preston, Paul. *The Triumph of Democracy in Spain.* London; New York: Methuen, 1986.
6. *Spain to 1992—Joining Europe's Mainstream.* EIU Economic Prospects Series, July, 1988.
7. Tamemes, Ramon. *Introduccion a la Economia Espanola.* Madrid: Alianza, 1985.

16

·········

NEGOTIATING IN NIGERIA

Introduction

Nigeria is one of the most economically progressive countries in sub-Saharan Africa. Economic development is a priority of the nation. Therefore, Nigeria presents a significant opportunity for investment.

Nigeria can be characterized by the diversity of its peoples. It is the most populous country in Africa. The people are divided by tribal groupings having differences in history, culture, and language. The tribes are geographically and culturally exclusive. There are three main ethnic groups in Nigeria. Somewhat isolated in the north, are the Fulani-Hausa who have a strong traditional Islamic culture. The Ibo of the southeast, as well as the Yoruba of the southwest, are predominately Christian and have been strongly influenced by Western thought. To further complicate matters, there are over 250 different languages and dialects spoken in Nigeria. In addition to economic development, one of the nation's main goals is to encourage better social integration.

Two types of nationalism developed in Nigeria. One is the modern brand that breeds civil servants, politicians, soldiers, and

201

professionals. This type has had a limited effect on unifying Nigeria because it is thinly spread throughout the population. Another much more pervasive form of nationalism exists within every Nigerian. It is traditional tribal loyalty but it serves to further divide the many groups.

The tribe is the basic sociological unit in Nigeria. It provides the individual with his sense of self, that is, his identity, his business and social relationships, and his rights and obligations as a member of the tribe. Tribalism is slowly breaking down, but it still exerts a significant influence on the members of Nigerian society.

The decade of the 1980s was harsh for Nigeria. Heavily dependent on oil revenues, Nigeria is vulnerable to world market prices. Low production and prices severely affected the economy in the early 1980s. The value of the Naire dropped as did the standard of living. Since 1986, the military government of General Ibrahim Babangida has implemented a Structural Adjustment Programme (SAP) under the guidance of the IMF. It is debatable how much the SAP has helped the economy. Servicing the debt of the country has been said to have wiped out any gains that had been made. In May 1989, anti-SAP riots broke out, and relief measures had to be brought in to soften the blow of the stringency of the SAP.

Historical Perspective

British influence in Nigeria was officially recognized in the late nineteenth century, although the nation did not actually become a colony until 1914. After World War II, the country moved gradually toward independence which it achieved in 1960. In 1963, Nigeria became a federal republic. The unique political traditions of the many peoples of Nigeria bred animosity and resulted in several uprisings and, hence, a somewhat unstable political system until the early 1980s.

The recent history of Nigeria resembles a tug-of-war game between military and civilian forces. In 1966 a military coup overthrew the constitutional monarchy. A period of intense violence between the eastern region and the northern and western regions followed. The eastern region seceded and formed the Republic of Biafra. A civil war ensued until 1970 when the eastern region surrendered.

The military ruled until 1975 when a bloodless coup occurred. In 1978, elections and a new constitution restored civilian rule. The government became interested in attracting investment at this time, but the oil crisis of the early 1980s led to a major decline in the economy and investment.

The end of 1983 saw another coup and the end of civilian rule. And again in 1985, the government switched hands, although still remaining under the control of the military. This last coup was lead by Major General Ibrahim Babangida who leads the government today.

Plans were made to transfer power to a civilian rule in 1990, but have been postponed until 1992. The future is uncertain, even though the present government is doing everything it can to ensure stability.

At the present, the economy is improving due to increased oil production coupled with higher prices. Also growth is expected in areas such as paint and chemicals, pharmaceuticals, petrochemicals, communications and transport. Even with these growth areas, inflation is expected to increase, and an overall lower growth rate is expected in 1990.

Nigeria has a possibility of becoming a semi-industrialized country through the petrochemical industry. Petrochemical companies are expected to produce the materials needed to make industrialized goods; however, investors are needed in areas that will use the products of the petrochemical plants. The government today wants to increase the flow of foreign capital.

Its history as a British colony influences Nigeria's attitude toward the West in general, and toward Western international business practices specifically. The nation sees its own economic development and industrialization in the context of a new economic order. It condemns the old order in which a few industrialized nations used exploitive, imperial patterns to dictate the terms of world trade.

The Twelve Negotiating Variables

Basic Concept of Negotiation Process

Negotiation is a way of life for Nigerians; many of them have been bargaining in the marketplace since childhood and have become skilled in the art. Society's emphasis on individual achievement has resulted in a view of negotiation as a competitive process. In the early stages, negotiation is characterized by cooperation. Offers, counteroffers, and informal meetings take up much time in this early part of the process. In the later stage of negotiation, conflict characterizes the atmosphere.

Business relations are based on trust, and business is personalized. As a result of these factors, the negotiation process is unhurried. Objectives are reached slowly through compromise. Centralization of decision-making power also slows down the process. In many cases, both in negotiations with the government and with private firms, the Nigerian negotiator may have to refer to his superior for direction. To expedite the process, a foreign businessman should be prepared to make decisions without lengthy referral to his own home office. It is important to remember that the Nigerians must also work within the framework of these obstacles and that if a foreigner becomes impatient, it could be detrimental to the negotiations.

A foreign businessman's impatience will probably be construed by the Nigerians as evidence of an imperial mentality and an attitude of superiority. Nigerians are extremely proud of their status as economic leaders among African nations, and it is unwise to risk offense with an unsuitable attitude.

A certain amount of racial prejudice against whites exists in Nigeria as a result of the country's colonial past, but sending a black negotiator may be construed as condescending. It is best, if at all possible, to send a black negotiator with a Caucasian. If it is not possible to send both, then send a Caucasian.

There is a "mobilization fee," or *dash*, that is usually paid to expedite business. Often it is the primary matter negotiated with foreigners.

Selection of Negotiators

In traditional Nigerian society, age is equated with wisdom and experience and perceived as being a tremendous advantage. It is an important criteria in the selection of a Nigerian representative. Sex is also somewhat important. Although women play a vital role in the Nigerian economy, males outrank females in accordance with traditional societal values.

Also considered in the selection of negotiators is status, experience, and personal attributes. A man's status and experience give him his business connections. His personality preserves these connections. Business and personal connections are crucial because the success of a business venture depends to a large degree on one's connections.

Importance is also attached to one's educational credentials. Because of the British influence, an individual with a general literary education is considered more capable than one knowledgeable in a particular subject or industry. A Ph.D. carries great weight.

Role of Individual Aspirations

While individual achievement is stressed, tribal loyalties remain high in all ethnic groups. Pressure is put on those who are financially successful to provide employment or financial support for their family or tribe. The predominance of *dash*, money paid to expedite services, illustrates this point. In many cases, these payments are used to support family or tribe members, not to increase personal gain. The feeling of responsibility to the tribe contributes a great deal to the practice of accepting or paying *dash.*

Theft is another issue that illustrates the relationship between individualistic behavior and tribal loyalty. Stealing from a member of one's tribe is condemned, but stealing from outsiders, particularly when the gains are shared with other members of the tribe, is condoned, at least socially.

A duality exists between the cultural pressures placed on individualistic behavior and those placed on tribal loyalty. The extent to which one of these behaviors predominates depends largely on the context of the situation.

Significance of Type of Issue

The relationship among members of the negotiation team as well as the relationship between opposing sides, takes precedence over issues of price and quality or other substantive concerns. Developing personal rapport between opposing sides is a key factor in the successful completion of negotiations.

Since the conduct of business is personalized, it is vital to select a representative who possesses an appropriate negotiation style. The Nigerians appreciate a slow approach that reflects respect and sincerity. They react unfavorably to hurriedness or the task-oriented cultures of the West. Haste conveys dishonesty and is seen as a manifestation of Western superiority.

One key factor influencing personal relationships is the emphasis placed on an individual's prestige. Prestige results from age, education, and experience. The individual is the main concern in negotiations in spite of the strong group affiliation evident in many other aspects of the society.

Middlemen play a pivotal role in the Nigerian business environment. All business is conducted through them and there is a significant dependence on their connections and on the ability to maintain those connections.

Complexity of Language

Emphasis is placed on non-verbal behavior. Foreign counterparts should show by listening carefully to what is being said that they are interested in the proceedings.

Concern with Protocol

The Nigerian business community conducts itself in a formal manner. A foreigner must observe formalities when working within this community; otherwise, he risks being thought of as having a casual attitude about the business at hand. The American manner of dressing is perceived as being casual, and therefore, insulting. It is vital that the foreign negotiator be well-dressed if he wishes to succeed.

Titles are extremely important and must be used, especially honorific titles of traditional leaders. People who hold university degrees commonly use these titles in business. Never use first names until invited to do so.

Since everything in Nigeria is personalized, it is crucial to conduct business in person. Transactions cannot be quick or impersonal. Initial introductions should be made by middlemen. Prior appointments should be made in dealing with members of the bureaucracy. Westerns should be prompt for meetings (even though Nigerians may not be) to show their seriousness and respect.

During negotiations some form of refreshment is almost always served and it must be accepted.

Politicking behind the scenes is frequent. Foreigners must be sensitive to the Nigerians' feelings in the negotiating process and socially. Since many colonial sensitivities remain, it is easy to give offense where none is intended. Courtesy and consideration must be consciously demonstrated; casual treatment is not acceptable.

The official language of Nigeria is English. More emphasis is placed on the spoken word than on the written. Meanings are subtle and internalized, and ambiguity is tolerated. Nigerians enjoy language and are impressed by eloquent usage. They may react adversely to a man who expresses himself poorly, carelessly, or colloquially. The best approach in most cases is for Westerns to be brief, precise, and to the point. A quiet, simple approach from a man with a good command of the language will earn the respect of the Nigerians and should aid in a successful conclusion to the negotiation.

Nature of the Persuasive Argument

One of the cultural characteristics of the Nigerians is their extroverted natures. They love language and they talk and argue vigorously. What may appear to outsiders as a heated argument may in reality merely be a healthy discussion.

Because accurate information is often lacking, experience, emotion, and intuition form the basis of a persuasive argument. Other factors include the respect accorded to age and education, the belief that the position of the individual is above the concerns of business, and the emphasis on personal loyalty and trust in business relationships.

An American entering negotiations should have maturity and experience. In stating his case, he should use a quiet approach and communicate in a clear, precise manner. Rather than relying on facts, figures, and statistics to sway his audience, he should speak in comparative terms.

Nigerians are proud of their country's status as a leading economic force in sub-Saharan Africa, and they are concerned with economic development. Foreign businessmen should show an interest in this goal and speak in terms of the role their investment can play in Nigeria's economic development and general social well-being.

Value of Time

Time is viewed as an abundant commodity in Nigeria and thus is of little importance because of its unlimited nature. Even the simplest transactions require a great deal of time. Tardiness to meetings (even of several hours) is common. In spite of this, it is crucial for foreign counterparts to make every effort to be punctual since this conveys a sense of importance to the proceedings. They must also be extremely patient when inevitable delays occur. An attitude of impatience will be met with hostility because it places the value of time above that of people and of business. A foreign counterpart should never hurry through the negotiations, even after a late start, as he may be suspected of cheating.

Bases of Trust

Business relationships evolve from personal relationships in which Nigerians spend much time in assessing their negotiating counterparts. Once friendship has developed with a foreign counterpart and his credentials and expertise have been examined, he is perceived in a favorable light.

Two different attitudes exist toward the sharing of information and communication. The traditional view dictates that since everyone is a competitor, one does not share information. However, attitudes are shifting toward a sharing of trade knowledge and the free flow of information especially among Nigerians trained in the United States.

It is vital for a foreign counterpart in Nigeria to maintain his integrity. It is important to be able to keep secrets to show that he can be trusted. Remnants of colonial hostility remain, and foreigners may be perceived as opportunists ready to further exploit Nigeria. Foreign counterparts should be prepared to meet with hostility. Nigeria's history as a colony has conditioned many Nigerians to resent and distrust white people, although the appointment of a black American may be seen as patronizing and evidence of an imperial mentality.

Risk-Taking Propensity

The Ibo and the Yoruba of the south are not risk-averse. The tradition of individual achievement among these peoples demands that the individual be willing to accept risk. This is evidenced by the predominance of *dash* in spite of the stiff penalties imposed by the government on this practice. In general, the peoples of sub-Saharan Africa are fatalists, and this too may have an impact on the perception of risk. Good fortune or bad is not necessarily seen as the outcome of a particular cause. Hence the Nigerian peoples, at least those of the south, are not risk-adverse, although they cannot be described as risk-seeking, but rather risk-accepting.

The attitude toward risk among the Fulani-Hausa of the north is different, possibly as a result of their Moslem heritage. They are risk-averse. There is a strong mistrust of innovation and a great reliance on precedent. The Fulani-Hausa are from a background in which highly centralized powers made it necessary for one to function within strict codes of law and behavior.

Internal Decision-Making Systems

Decision making is extremely centralized. There is almost no delegation of authority. The American concept of participative management does not exist. The authority figure in an organization holds the key position. His status in the organization is that of complete leadership; he controls completely and gives focus to all phases of activity or negotiation. Subordinates look to him for commands and do not take initiative or perform a task without explicit orders. If a leader should fail in his role of command, he loses the respect of his subordinates. His position of power and prestige cannot be shared without being diluted which would cause him to lose stature. This applies to all levels of an organization. Most private enterprises as well as the bureaucracy function within a strict hierarchical environment.

Form of Satisfactory Agreement

Nigerians place more emphasis on the spoken word rather than on the written word, although the practice is to pursue written agreements, a practice imposed by the British during colonial times. The culmination to a negotiation lies in reaching an understanding between parties, not producing a legally enforceable document. Agreements, whether written or oral are regarded as flexible with changing circumstances.

Concluding Scenario
Investment in Nigeria?

Although foreign investors have been encouraged to enter into negotiations with Nigeria, they should consider how far this encouragement extends. Investment is sought in the petrochemical industry, mining, and manufacturing. There are three types of businesses in Nigeria. Businesses that are wholly owned by Nigerians; businesses that are 60 percent Nigerian; and businesses that are 40 percent Nigerian. In order to invest in Nigeria, a corporation must follow their rules. It is only in the last few years that joint ventures have even been allowed.

The main incentives are tax incentives, although until recently, tax incentives were not favorable to foreign investment. Since 1987, exemptions for dividends have been created in agriculture. More changes have occurred such as the relaxation of laws concerning reinvestment of dividends, and more changes are expected to occur in the future.

In the light of political instability over the last thirty years and the distressful economic situation in the 1980s, one would be wise to research completely issues concerning investment in Nigeria.

Investment must be considered in the light of the Nigerian peoples as well. Because of their diverse culture, attitudes, and history, an investor should look at each situation individually and with a willingness to learn.

There are some cultural characteristics that hold true to some degree across ethnic and regional divisions. Most Nigerians are ambitious, competitive, and industrious. They are patient, accepting of differences among people, and ready to accept a challenge.

Foreigners all face the same challenge when conducting business in Nigeria. Negotiations are time consuming and require a unique type of representative to cope with the difficulties. Large prepayments are required for services. Furthermore delays always occur in all phases of business, payment, delivery, and administrative decision making.

Americans, however, have several advantages in business in Nigeria. They have language in common, plus a good reputation for delivery, quality, and price. Americans were not colonists of Nigeria, but their treatment of black Americans is a cause for tension.

Nigeria is a nation rich in resources and opportunity for the business willing to work within the unique cultural framework of the country.

References and Suggested Readings

1. Ghauri, Perez N. "Negotiating with Firms in Developing Countries: Two Case Studies," Industrial Marketing Management, Volume 17: Number 1, February, 1988. pp. 49-53.
2. Harris, Philip R. and Robert T. Moran, *Managing Cultural Differences*, Houston, Texas: Gulf Publishing Company, 1987.
3. Lanier, Alison R., *Update: Nigeria*, New York City, New York: Overseas Briefing Associates, 1978.
4. Overseas Business Reports, International Marketing Information Series, *Marketing in Nigeria*, United States Department of Commerce, International Trade Administration, 1988.
5. The Parker Pen Company, *Do's and Taboos Around the World*, Elmsford, New York: The Benjamin Company, 1985.
6. Schwartz Jr., Frederick A.O., *Nigeria: The Tribes, the Nation, or the Race—The Politics of Independence*, Cambridge, Massachusetts: The M.I.T. Press, 1965.
7. Schwarz, Walter, *Nigeria*, New York City, New York: Frederick A. Praeger, 1968.
8. Weiss, Stephen and William Stripp, "Negotiating with Foreign Businesspersons: An Introduction for Americans with Propositions on Six Cultures," New York University, New York City, New York, February, 1985.

17

....

NEGOTIATING IN MEXICO

Introduction

In Mexico's long and rich history, perhaps one of the most important dates of modern times was February 4, 1990. On this date, Mexican government officials and fifteen representatives of creditor banks signed the financial package allowing Mexico to reduce the principal and interest on its debt and to receive enough new credit to recapture its healthy economic growth. Mexico's foreign debt was decreased by 20.5 billion dollars. With international co-responsibility, Mexico has made history and has guaranteed its presence in the twenty-first century. The debt crisis that exploded in 1982 has been resolved, and the Mexican government and its people now face a new challenge—to grow to new heights in economic, social and political arenas.

Historical Perspective

During the age of discovery, Spanish fleets ventured across the virtually uncharted Atlantic to discover the exotic, unique and rich land and people that is today Mexico. The Europeans colonized Mexico nearly a century before they reached North America. Mexico City, then called Tenochtitian, was the largest city on the continent and one of the grandest in the world. The Aztecs, one in a long line of Indian civilizations, inhabited Tenochtitian and ruled over an empire that stretched to what is now Central America, and traded as far north as modern Arizona and New Mexico. A highly civilized and inventive society, the Aztecs were skilled in the arts, science and mathematics.

This group of people was conquered by the Spanish in 1519, under the leadership of Hernan Cortes. The Spanish ruled Mexico, which was called "New Spain," for 300 years. During this time the Spaniards destroyed many of the pagan temples, enslaved the people, imposed European rule and the Roman Catholic religion, and superimposed the Castilian language. The colonizers also carried off fabulous treasures from this vast and rich territory. The colonial period concentrated on mining and cattle raising, and international trade was restricted to Spain. The Spanish colonists and their descendants grew wealthy from the fruits of the Indians' labor.

Mexico's increased economic growth and continued development of a home market in the eighteenth century, contributed to rapid social change. In 1810, New Spain erupted against the tyrannous Spaniards. Father Miguel Hidalgo y Costilla led an uprising of Indians and mestizos that began the eleven year war for independence. Despite its tumultuous beginning and lack of planning, Mexico gained its independence from Spain.

Three hundred years of tightly controlled Spanish colonization was followed by decades of struggles for political power and slow economic development. In 1836, Texas, which had been part of the Mexican empire, was ceded to the United States. In the Mexican-American War (1846-48), Mexico lost half of its territory, including New Mexico, Arizona, and California to the United States.

It was not until the end of the nineteenth century that thirty years of internal peace was achieved in Mexico under Porfirio Diaz. During this time the great haciendas, large land areas used for cattle raising and farming, reached their peak. However, the Mexican Revolution of 1910 almost destroyed the scene of some of the most dramatic struggles of the twentieth century.

Since 1940, there has been economic progress and political stability in Mexico under the PRI (Partido Revolucionario Institucional). The PRI has come to be the most powerful institution after the presidency. Social tensions were calmed in the 1970s as a result of unprecedented economic growth and prosperity from the discovery of the massive Chiapas oil field. Mexico is today the world's fourth largest producer of oil, and the fifth largest reserve base worldwide. Oil and oil derivatives are by far the most important of Mexico's merchandise exports, although their contributions to total earnings have fallen in recent years.

Mexico is one of the world's leading silver producers as well. Since the arrival of the Spaniards some 450 years ago, Mexican ore has been extracted and processed around the globe.

Tourism is also another fundamental source of economic wealth for the country. Mexico offers sunshine, warm beaches, mountain scenery, ancient ruins, colorful towns and cities, and vibrant culture to its growing number of tourists.

Mexican cultural, social, and political life reflects the cumulation of 450 years of influences of Spanish, Aztec, and Mayan civilizations. The people of Mexico are striving to make their country a part of the industrialized world. They must deal with several powerful juxtapositions in their society today—the new and the old, wealth and poverty, formality and disorder. However, as history has shown, Mexicans are a resilient people, capable of adjustment and change. The challenge of the future can only pale in comparison with their long and chaotic past. If existence is based on the survival of the fittest, than Mexico should outlive many a country.

The Twelve Negotiating Variables

Basic Concept of Negotiation Process

Negotiating in Mexico is a complex and a drawn out procedure. Negotiations cover several stages and may appear to move slowly. First, the parties involved must determine if they, as individuals or organizations, can do business together. Establishing a warm working relationship with one's counterparts is essential, and facilitates the negotiation.

The process itself will use distributive bargaining tactics. Mexicans adhere to the concept of "limited goods" and assume competitive postures. This does not necessarily entail openly verbalizing disagreements. However, Mexicans usually are skilled at avoiding confrontation and loss of face and see little value in frank exchange, preferring behind the scenes bargaining.

At the negotiation table, because of past historical context, a Mexican negotiator is wary of being taken advantage of by an American *gringo*. Mexican pride, *machismo* will not allow this to happen. It is important for a negotiator to be sensitive to any real or implied messages contrary to Mexican self-esteem.

Connections in Mexico are important and a bribe can grease the wheels of action effectively. The government has a heavy influence in private business matters. Permits are required for just about every business transaction. As a result a government official might elicit a bit of *mordida* to complete the transaction. A negotiator needs to examine his moral standards and understand his company's by-laws to react to this common practice.

Selection of Negotiators

Negotiators are selected primarily on status. Family connections, personal or political influence and education are critical. Hence the importance of *ubicacion* ("where one is plugged into the system") becomes evident. The use of paternal and maternal surnames helps one to discern familial connections and is an important factor in determining one's standing in the community or corporation.

Mexican negotiators tend to be high level, male, and well connected. They are also rhetoricians and tend to rely on the force of their personalities. Loyalty to one's *patron* or boss might be more highly valued than expertise. However, the importance of an employee's loyalty to his boss and company is eroding, being replaced with a trend towards "self-loyalty."

Role of Individual Aspirations

Whether Mexicans are individualists or collectivists seems to depend on the social arena. In business, and with other men, Mexicans tend to be competitive, set on pursuing individual goals and needs for their personal recognition. Often they feel they owe loyalty to their *patron*, but they also seek to project a public image of significance and power. Individual aspiration may take the form of political maneuvering and ingratiating oneself with the right people.

In family and social relationships, there seems to be a collective orientation, in which family units may contain a variety of friends and relatives.

Concern with Protocol

Mexican culture is dominated by courtesy, dignity, tact, and diplomacy. Protocol is important. Social competence is as critical as technical competence.

In the business environment, expected behaviors must be followed. These include ritual handshaking and greeting of counterparts. Some convivial remark should accompany a greeting such as asking about the person's health or family.

Etiquette also governs the use of first names and the two forms of "you": *usted* (formal) and *tu* (familiar). The former is always used in business contracts. In business conversation it is polite to address a person by his title. The *tu* is reserved for those people whom one would address by their first name. It would be a breach of etiquette to use *tu* until a senior person has indicated that would be in order.

When a negotiator exchanges greetings using both maternal and paternal surnames, he should also exchange business cards. The business card should include the negotiator's academic titles. Academic credentials can gain instant respect.

Negotiations must include mutual business lunch invitations. More deals and agreements are reached over lunch in Mexico than in any office or conference room. Mexican negotiators seem to feel most at home in informal settings where personal relationships are given a chance to develop and grow.

Significance of Type of Issue

For Mexicans, relationship-based and personal/internal issues tend to predominate and affect the negotiations. Mexicans emphasize the social and personal aspects of their relationships with the people they encounter, including businessmen. At the outset of a meeting, conversation is social and personal to establish rapport. The foundation for future dealings is set by being sensitive and warm, but formal and courteous.

Many Mexicans resent what they see as a long history of unfair treatment by the North Americans. In negotiating, this issue may come to the fore as a question of personal honor or dignity, and often presents a problem within the Mexican team.

Complexity of Language

Communicative context is formed by body language and emotional cues, not just diction. Mexicans communicate with hand movements, physical contact and emotional expressions. The following are culturally specific gesture interpretations: hands do not belong in pockets while a businessman is in public; hands on hips signal a challenge or a threat; and hands should be on top of the table especially during meals.

All Latin American cultures embrace closeness. People stand close to each other, sit close to each other, and touch each other. When talks go well, Mexicans commonly lay a hand on the shoulder of their counterpart. One should not attempt to withdraw from this gesture. This is a positive signs of warm, personal, and attentive interaction.

Frankness and openness might be viewed with suspicion since a Mexican negotiator might have a tendency to say what a counterpart wishes to hear or give evasive replies.

Nature of Persuasive Argument

Emotional arguments that are overly dramatic and patriotic are considered persuasive. Along these lines, there is the concept of *proyectismo* (constructing plans without critical analysis and assuming in time all will be accomplished). Perhaps much of this stems from the twin origins of Mexican culture: the Indian, based on magic and superstition, and the Spanish, based on imposition, dogma, and faith.

Mexicans may also be persuaded by the rhetoric of experience rather than emotions. They may emphasize general principles and minimize problem solving.

Value of Time

There is a relaxed polychronic attitude toward time. Although time is a concern, Mexicans do not allow schedules to interfere with experiences involving their family or friends. The culture is people rather than task-oriented.

Mexicans recognize that North Americans have a different perception of time. They find the urgency to "get to the point" quite distasteful and ill-mannered. An appointment that must be met with promptness is called a *cita inglesa*—an English appointment. It is best for foreigners to be flexible about time. Time commitments are considered desirable objectives but not binding promises.

In Mexico time is plentiful; detailed plans cannot affect the course of nature. Mexican negotiators see little urgency in efforts to conclude an agreement.

Bases of Trust

Evaluations of trustworthiness are based initially on intuition and then later on one's past record. Negotiations often take place within a generally trusting atmosphere. Never expect Mexicans to trust you during the first meeting you conduct with them. However, if a situation arises that causes mistrust, trust may be lost indefinitely. Trust must develop through a series of frequent and warm interpersonal transactions, either socially or business oriented.

Risk-Taking Propensity

Mexicans tend to be risk-avoidant. They will try to work something out to avoid risk as much as possible. Mexicans tend to be very pessimistic in any situation in which there is some amount of risk.

Internal Decision-Making Systems

Decision making is highly centralized in government, companies, and within negotiating teams. Mexican leaders tend to make decisions without concern for consensus. Subordinates' abilities are not highly valued. At the same time, subordinates accept their leaders' broad use of power.

Decision-making power does not simply come with position, however. Individuals with *palanca* (leverage) tend to be well positioned, expressive, and forceful with their opinions and decisions.

Form of Satisfactory Agreement

The only way to be certain that a business agreement has been reached in Mexico is with a written document. Oral statements that everything is fine are positive signs, but little value should be placed on them. These oral signals may serve only to save feelings, and a negative decision might come later in the mail. Agreements in Mexico fall under the Civil Code, the Commercial Code, or the Law of Commercial Companies. A qualified attorney should assure completeness and validity of the agreement.

Concluding Scenario
Mexico's New Challenge—Growth

With the recent debt agreement, Mexico has a brighter and more opportunistic view of the future. There will be more opportunities for foreign companies interested in what Mexico has to offer. In the past, certain restrictions made it difficult for foreigners to participate in stock investments in Mexico. However, under new foreign investment rules (as of May 1989) almost all trade barriers have been eliminated and foreigners are allowed to purchase almost any stock. According to one Mexican source, now is a good time to invest in Mexico. The lower inflation rates and the privatizing of business, among other factors, have brought confidence back to Mexico. Today there is more trust in Mexico, and Mexico, in a sense, may have more trust in the world. The new positive image that has surfaced after long and arduous internal and external struggles is heartily welcomed among the Mexicans and the global community.

To be successful in business negotiations, however, one must have a general understanding of the Mexican culture and the intricacies of its business culture as well. The historical perspective and the twelve variables as presented here give a solid and thorough base for doing business in Mexico. Like a fine gourmet meal, the ingredients for a successful business venture are available. With some careful measuring and timing these ingredients may be combined, prepared and presented by the nations of the world in their dealings with the Mexicans to ensure a satisfying economic entrée for all parties involved.

References and Suggested Readings

1. Bender, Mathew. *Doing Business in Mexico.* New York, New York: Southern Methodist University, 1987.
2. Condon, John C. *Good Neighbors: Communicating With The Mexicans.* Yarmouth, Maine: Intercultural Press, 1985.
3. ———. *Guidelines for Mexicans and North Americans.* Yarmouth, Maine: Intercultural Press, 1980.
4. Knippers Black, Jan., (ed.). *Latin America: Its Problems and Its Promise.* Boulder, CO: Westview Press, 1984.
5. Kras, Eva S. *Management in Two Cultures: Bridging the Gap Between U.S. and Mexican Managers.* Yarmouth, Maine: Intercultural Press, 1988.
6. Marett, Robert. *Mexico.* London: Thames & Hudson, 1971.
7. "Mexico." United States Department of State, Bureau of Public Affairs, December, 1985.
8. Paz, Octavio. *El Laberinto de la Soledad.* México: Fondo de Cultura Económica, 1959.
9. ———. *The Other Mexico: Critique of the Pyramid.* New York: Grove Press, Inc., 1972.
10. Riding, Alan. *Distant Neighbors: A Portrait of the Mexicans.* New York: Vintage Books, 1986.
11. Ross, Stanley R. *Mexican-U.S. Relations: An Historical Perspective.* Doubleday, 1983.

18

....

NEGOTIATING IN BRAZIL

Introduction

From the lush rain forests of the Amazon to the modern cities of Brasilia and Sao Paulo, Brazil is a country rich in heritage and natural resources.

Brazil is more an enigma than an entity. Because of its peculiar combination of wealth and industrial might in the south, Third-world poverty and hunger in the northeast, urban wealth and sophistication in Sao Paulo and Rio de Janeiro, wildlife preserves in the Pantanal, and aboriginal tribes in the Amazon territories and interior, the Brazilian cultural continuum includes the polar opposites of the social spectrum, as well as every variation in between.

In March 1990, Brazil installed Fernando Collor de Mello, representing the center right, as president. He defeated the left-wing candidate in a vote split that speaks acutely to the division of the Brazilian people and their assessment of the problems that have crippled their economy during the decade of the 1980s. The two most critical problems of the immediate future that the new president must handle are inflation and corruption at the state level.

President Collor de Mello plans to streamline the state apparatus that has been spending more than it collects in taxes. He plans to accomplish this in part by reducing the number of government ministries. Additionally, it is likely that many state companies will be privatized in an effort to make them more competitive and efficient. Other probable economic measures are a reduction in tariffs to eliminate the excessive protection of the Brazilian industry, allowing it to compete more effectively in the global market. Also being considered is a proposal to decentralize the debt negotiations allowing the individual debtor institutions to negotiate on a case-by-case basis with their respective creditors. By doing this, the government would no longer guarantee all of the debt.

Brazil's success in the export market has been phenomenal. In 1988, it had reached a $19 billion surplus in its trade account. During 1989, the export levels were lower because of the increasing volume of imports and the overvaluation of the cruzado, which has been lagging behind the level of inflation.

Brazil has enormous industrial potential but President Collor de Mello must solve its economic problems.

Historical Perspective

Discovered by the Portuguese navigator, Pedro Alvares Cabral in 1500, Brazil remained a Portuguese possession until 1822 when it became an independent monarchy, and later, a republic in 1889. Since then, Brazil's history has revealed much political upheaval with frequent changes of presidential rule. Rising debt and internal turmoil greatly affected Brazil's outlook.

Brazil's economic development has been characterized by booms and busts created in part by export cycles. Between the colonial period and the first century of its independence, Brazil became one of the leading producers of sugar. Sugarcane was, and still is, abundantly harvested in the north-eastern states of Recife and Salvador. The extraction of gold and diamonds from the mines of the state of Minas Gerais created the second boom in Brazil's economic history. Coffee production caused the third boom in the early nineteenth century. Brazil continues to be one of the leading producers of coffee. Spectacular rubber production caused the fourth boom in the Amazon region between 1850 and 1920. It was followed by a bust in the early 1920s as more efficient yields were produced in Southeast Asia.

The movement towards rapid industrialization was started after the 1930s when the depression hit Brazil's coffee-based export sector. Since then, the government became the chief sponsor for building and modernization of the industrial sector. This has accounted for tremendous growth rates, causing many to label the country the "Brazilian miracle" in the decades of the fifties, sixties, and seventies.

During the 1980s, Brazil gained international attention with the extensive burning of its tropical rain forests. This destruction followed the construction of new roads that provided access to impenetrable areas for cattle ranchers and lumber companies. In addition to the destruction of animal and plant life, it is believed that the emission of carbon dioxide from the fires has caused incalculable damage to the earth's ozone layer. Brazil finally gave in to international pressure and placed extensive environmental controls on the developing industries and established measures to protect the rain forests.

Despite their recent economic and environmental problems, Brazilians are proud of their achievements and want to be recognized as one of the world's great industrial powers. To many, Brazil's history and industrial structure appears similar to other Latin American countries. In reality, however, they are different. Linguistically as well as culturally, Brazil is distinct in Latin America in that it draws from the Portuguese heritage, rather than from the Spanish culture.

The Twelve Negotiating Variables

Basic Concept of the Negotiation Process

In a society that prizes verbal facility, wit, and eloquence, discussions are not a means to achieve an end, but an end in themselves. Whereas an American or a European might call a negotiating round "productive," a Brazilian might well describe it as "enjoyable." The negotiating process is often valued more, or just as much as, the end result. Discussions in Brazil tend to be lively, heated, and inviting.

Brazilian negotiators prefer to suggest, rather than to impose their will. This causes the entire negotiating process to take longer than usual, causing some North Americans to view this approach as inefficient and time-consuming. In contrast, Brazilians regard the North American approach to negotiating as overly blunt, and lacking consideration for the human aspect of the process. More importance is placed on the relationships of people at the table than on the issue being discussed, and unless a lively give and take occurs between the parties, there is no rapport as far as Brazilians are concerned.

Selection of Negotiators

Considering Brazil's strongly-defined, hierarchial society, in which a person's position is determined by the social class he is born into, it is not surprising to see a Brazilian negotiating team composed of people of academic and social distinction. The attitude of Brazilians toward culture is not one of practical necessity or moral value, but one of class or distinction.

A Brazilian negotiator is likely to come from an elite background, have a private school education, high academic merit, and the capability of subjecting his counterparts to the pomp of his erudition.

Personal attributes like affability, charm, and oratory powers, good social and political connections, and seniority in an organization are important considerations for selection to a negotiating team. Absence of any of these has to be compensated or offset by strength of other characteristics.

Work performance and accomplishments are increasingly replacing other qualifications in Brazil today, but individuals with good track records in the organization are more likely to form the support team rather than the actual negotiating group. Academics or professors are often found on a Brazilian negotiating team because the country is obsessed with academic prestige. Such appointments are more for decoration than participation.

Most companies in Brazil are privately owned. It is common to find more companies that are managed by the actual owners, rather than managers representing the owners. If a negotiator is dealing with a small privately-held company, it is important to discern if the manager is also an owner, because this will effect his motivation for the negotiation.

Individual Aspirations

Although the Brazilians are a gregarious people, with strong family attachments, they tend to be individualistic in their professional life. Individual performance during a negotiating round is considered more important than the team effort. They seldom, if at all, depend on each other for support during the negotiation. A Brazilian makes every effort to outshine his colleagues, without making it obvious.

A considerable amount of machismo still exists though it is not as acceptable today as in the past. Industrialization in the last decades, coupled with the entrance of women in the workplace, has changed the perception of working women, but it is still uncommon for them to be in the senior levels of management. Men in Brazilian society have more authority than women and are given greater liberties.

Concern with Protocol

The Brazilian approach to negotiations is one of formality and informality. On the one hand, Brazilians are class conscious and aware of the social hierarchy and the proper demeanor and formality that is the expected norm. Conversely, they use the social situation informally to get to know their counterparts to facilitate the negotiations.

Formality is evident in the importance Brazilians place on dressing fashionably. Individuals who do not dress fashionably are considered less interesting and less authoritative. Foreign counterparts are expected to be stylish in language, attire, and attitude.

Deference to age, seniority, and status are essential in the Brazilian business setting. Business meetings are conducted with pomp and ceremony. Work routines and chains of command are strictly codified and adhered to.

It is customary at the beginning of the negotiation to address each other with *senor*, or mister, followed by the surname. If a person has a title, it is used instead of *senor*. As negotiations progress, counterparts usually address each other on a first name basis. A handshake accompanies an introduction with mutual eye contact, smiles, and a mutual nod. When joining or leaving the negotiating session, a Brazilian will shake hands. This is of extreme importance as it is seen as a sign of mutual respect.

Brazilians bestow lavish hospitality on delegates after meetings in an effort to establish a comfortable social climate.

Brazilians spend much time ensuring that the proper tone is set for negotiating and do not cut corners in establishing a trust relationship. These deliberate steps are considered considerate and courteous by some, and formal and inefficient by some North Americans.

Significance of Type of Issue

Compatibility of styles and mutual trust are the primary issues of concern for Brazilians in approaching the negotiating process. They often prefer to negotiate with people they know. When dealing with people they don't know, they are cautious and attempt to develop the relationship before they proceed with the negotiation.

Substantive issues seem irrelevant. What is beyond the present hardly exists. Resignation to nature arouses disdain for details, truth, science, and reality. What appeals to them is abstraction; the emphasis on being rather than becoming. Even education in Brazil has been oriented toward understanding, not changing, man's place in the universe. Even today, in many universities, the largest enrollments are found in courses of philosophy and history.

A high-level Brazilian team seldom concerns itself with plans and much less with details. All of that is relegated to subordinate teams. Discussions center on general situations and establishing rapport. If a common profitable ground is discovered, and if a good relationship is established, the Brazilian team has justified its purpose.

Complexity of Language

Brazilian society is based on a relatively high cultural context. More subtlety is used to convey meaning and intent than in the United States where documentation and specifications are prized.

Brazilians resolve difficulties with a high-context, less-direct approach. Their meandering manner is an expression of interest and concern not a means of avoidance. To assure successful negotiations, low-context communicators should have a high degree of patience towards ambiguity and learn how to slowly define the terms of an agreement.

Direct eye contact is a must, and in a culture that has little or no personal space, ideas are often reinforced with touch. Tugging the earlobe is a sign of approval, but the American "A-O.K." sign, formed by making a circle with the thumb and forefinger, is an obscene gesture in Brazil.

Nature of Persuasive Argument

Intuition and sound common sense are parts of the Brazilian approach to persuasion. Because of the emphasis on interpersonal relationships and the indirect approach to working toward a solution, Brazilians are more likely to be persuaded by their relationships with the people involved and their understanding of them. When arguing, Brazilians resort to appealing to one's sensibility and tend to color their negotiations with a touch of emotionalism. Arguments are persuasive, not because they are based on statistics and figures, but because they are based on apparently sound common sense and are made with fervor and sincerity.

Inference, assumptions, and tradition are likely to play a part in persuasion. Inference is used because it is more subtle than fact, assumptions because they are inherent in human nature and difficult to avoid. Tradition is used because Brazilian society is defined by a culturally consistent past. It is not a renowned melting pot and is more unified under one religion than is the United States.

Value of Time

Brazilians recognize that time cannot be dominated by man; therefore, they are resigned to it. Unlike people from some low-context cultures, they do not try to capture time within the confines of hours, minutes, and seconds.

Brazilians are polychronic; that is, they are more concerned about the involvement of people and the completion of a transaction rather than the adherence to preset schedules. They are able to have many things happening at the same time. This is not to say that they don't care about time, but they have a flexible attitude towards it. Many Brazilians believe that human beings are more important than an abstract schedule. Monochronic cultures like the North Americans equate promptness with success; not so in Brazil. A junior person, however, must never keep a senior person waiting.

Patience is necessary when negotiating with Brazilians. Impatience or any attempt to bind an agreement within a time frame may seem inconsequential to a Brazilian, and he may regard it as compulsiveness. Brazilians have their innate rhythm, and foreigners should accept it with serenity. In Brazil, everything is slower and takes longer than anticipated. Events often start later than scheduled.

Bases of Trust

Although they are known for their hospitality, Brazilians do not open themselves easily or totally. To gain trust, a foreigner needs more than credentials; he must be willing to commit to a long-term relationship. In North America, trust can be instantaneous if the person has the required skills. In Brazil trust is built slowly. A satisfactory experience with Brazilians in the past, will generally ensure trust for the future.

Risk-Taking Propensity

Brazilians are basically risk-averse. In a society where social hurdles must be overcome to achieve prominence, a successful person will not jeopardize his position. Brazilians are basically complacent, and view work as only a part of one's life. They are comfortable in a strict hierarchial structure with clearly defined roles.

In negotiating with Brazilians, it is futile to define monetary gains as an incentive to taking risks. Though they are in business to make money, they would rather play safe and retain what they have than lose in an attempt to gain more. Other motivators like power, prestige, and recognition are more effective in Brazil.

Internal Decision-Making Systems

A highly bureaucratic decision-making system usually goes hand in hand with a strictly defined, class conscious, hierarchial society. Such a system tends to slow down the decision-making process, especially when time has little significance. During the negotiation, decisions are seldom made by an individual. Middle-level negotiators or managers act as intermediaries between higher levels of the company and the negotiating team. Within this framework, middle level executives are expected to follow orders and to suggest rather than take charge.

Form of Satisfactory Agreement

Brazilians distrust lawyers and at the same time look to them to protect their interests. Their innate cordiality prompts Brazilians to conclude a negotiation with a handshake and a word of honor. This, however, is at the higher levels of negotiations. Once an agreement has been reached, lawyers work with the subordinate teams to document and formalize the agreement. This is not surprising in view of the conflicting traits in the Brazilian character of hospitality and distrust.

Concluding Scenario
Can Foreign Negotiators See the Forest Through the Trees?

Before conducting business in Brazil, foreigners must understand how Brazilians perceive work and relationships. One major factor in negotiation is that social relationships play a major role in business. An intermediary is essential in establishing rapport with business associates. Contacts are important; many jobs are gained through friends and family. "Cold calls" are not successful because salespeople and business executives usually have to be referred by a friend. When doing business or negotiating in Brazil for the first time, a business should hire a lawyer. Many North American consulting companies can recommend a good one. He can act as the liaison between you and your counterparts and help ensure a more efficient and successful outcome to your endeavors.

Avoid confrontations and choose the road of conciliation to resolve any business conflicts. Patience pays, and it is important to learn to deal with ambiguity because information is usually exchanged in an indirect way. Finally, take a relaxed view of time. Always remember that you are dealing in a different cultural context where time has other meanings.

Doing business in Brazil can be frustrating for all parties involved. However, if foreigners look beyond their perceptions and learn to understand and respect the Brazilian culture, they will have a better opportunity for successful negotiations in Brazil.

References and Suggested Readings

1. "Brazil Country Report" No. 4-1989. *The Economist Intelligence Unit.* London: Business International, 1989.
2. Ewbank, Thomas. *Life in Brazil.* New York: Harper and Brothers, 1971.
3. Harrison, Phyllis A. *Behaving Brazilian.* Cambridge: Newbury House Publishers, 1983.
4. Poppino, Rollie E. *Brazil: The Land and People.* New York: Oxford University Press, 1968.
5. Rodrigues, Jose Honorio. *The Brazilians.* Trans. Ralph Edward Dimmick. Austin: University of Texas Press, 1969.
6. Smith, Lynn T., *Brazil: People and Institutions.* Baton Rouge: Louisiana State University Press, 1972.
7. *South America, Central America and the Caribbean.* 1st ed. London: Europe Publications Limited, 1986.
8. Wagley, Charles. *An Introduction to Brazil.* New York: Columbia University Press, 1971.

THE INTERNATIONAL NEGOTIATOR'S PASSPORT TO SUCCESS

If there is one word to differentiate the *skillful* from the *not skillful* international business negotiators, it is preparation. Preparation is not everything, but it is of great significance. However, all negotiators prepare. Skillful negotiators prepare differently. This book is about preparing to profile your negotiating counterparts. This final section provides a checklist that can be photocopied and carried with one's passport. We wish you success.

The information presented is based on The International Negotiator's Passport to Success compiled by Robert Moran. The usefulness of the passport has already been demonstrated by many persons. We recommend that a number of Passports to Success be made available, and one be completed for each business trip. Printed copies that can be folded to easily fit with your actual passport are available.[1]

Experience has shown that it takes from one to several hours to complete the preparation. Experience has also shown that it is better to complete the preparation with other team members.

Permission is given to photocopy the following pages.

---

[1]To obtain a copy of the *International Negotiator's Passport to Success* write to: Robert T. Moran, Ph.D., 5000 N. Wilkinson Rd., Scottsdale, Arizona 85253.

Preparation for International Business Negotiations

Skillful international negotiators work toward *mutual* benefits, while recognizing and managing cultural differences.

Review the first eight points from your perspective. This task is to be completed individually.

Question 1   What are the purposes of the negotiation in general? What are the purposes for this meeting?

     2   What departments and individuals are involved? Previous sales? Previous contacts?

     3   List the main issues to be negotiated.

     4   What are your specific objectives during the upcoming meeting. Write them on a sheet of paper.

     5   Review all letters, telexes, and other exchanges of information.

     6   Who will make the presentations? Who, on your team, has excellent language skills?

     7   Do you need an interpreter?

     8   What are the roles of your team members? What phases will the negotiation pass through?

     9   Now review the above eight points from your negotiating counterpart's perspective.

Team Preparation

This part of the preparation is to be completed with the other members of your team.

1. Decide on the roles of each member. Who are the technical experts, the commercial experts, the skillful negotiators?
2. Identify five strengths and weaknesses of each member.
3. Clarify roles and responsibilities of each member before, during, and after a negotiation.
4. Discuss and agree on objectives, strategy, and approaches.

Cooperative Policy

Review with each team member.

Team Training

1. Develop close association with each other.
2. Share negotiation experiences.
3. Discuss how each looks at negotiation:

- an on-going process of developing a relationship? or
- a problem-solving discussion of our business objectives? or
- a process where we have a mutual interest in finding a solution that is favorable for both parties

Discuss how to accomplish above:

_____

_____

_____

_____

Review of Terms

Review with each team member.

Strategy: A well thought out game plan; a planned effort to achieve a set of goals or objectives.

Tactics: A set of acts performed for gaining an advantage in terms of positions envisioned in a plan.

Maneuvers: Unanticipated movements aimed at securing tactical gains.

Discussion of the strategy:

_____

_____

_____

_____

Summary of the Twelve Variables for our Negotiations

Complete using culture specifics presented in the book or do additional research.

1. WHAT NEGOTIATING IS:
   distributive bargaining/joint problem-solving/debate/contingency bargaining/nondirective-discussion
2. HOW NEGOTIATORS ARE SELECTED:
   knowledge/negotiating experience/personal attirbutes/status
3. ISSUES DISCUSSED ARE:
   substantive/relationship-based/procedural/personal-internal
4. PROTOCOL:
   informality ⟵——————⟶ formality
5. CONTEXT (use of language):
   low ⟵——————⟶ high
6. HOW ARGUMENTS ARE SOLVED:
   empirical reason/experience/dogma/emotion/intuition
7. TEAM MEMBERS ARE:
   individuals ⟵——————⟶ group
8. HOW TRUST IS ESTABLISHED:
   external sanctions/past record/intuition
9. RISK TAKING:
   high ⟵——————⟶ low
10. TIME USE:
    monochronic ⟵——————⟶ polychronic
11. DECISIONS ARE:
    authoritative ⟵——————⟶ consensus
12. AGREEMENT IS:
    contractual ⟵——————⟶ implicit

Their Perception of Our People

Stereotypes are exaggerations of reality, but are frequently accepted as fact. Completing "Their Perception of our People" may give you a sense of what they may say "behind your backs."

Step One:
Place a check on the left of the word if you believe the word reflects how your negotiating counterpart sees you.

Step Two:
Place a check on the right of the words that express the way you want to be perceived by your negotiating counterparts.

Step Three:
Review the differences. Now, formulate a strategy to change their perceptions so that they will perceive you as you want to be perceived, that is, make a style shift to be perceived as you wish to be perceived.

THEIR PERCEPTION OF OUR PEOPLE

How do they "see" you?		How do you want them to "see" you?
	CURIOUS	
	TOLERANT	
	AGGRESSIVE	
	GENEROUS	
	COLD	
	HUMOROUS	
	IMAGINATIVE	
	SUBMISSIVE	
	FRIENDLY	
	IDEALISTIC	
	ACTIVE	
	WARM	
	RESPECTFUL	

INSECURE
CRITICAL
REALISTIC
PASSIVE
SERIOUS
INSENSITIVE
CONFIDENT
DISHONEST
SINCERE
DOMINEERING
SUPERFICIAL

STYLE SHIFT

_____

_____

_____

_____

BIBLIOGRAPHY
Culture and Behavior

Adler, Nancy J. *International Dimensions of Organizational Behavior.* Belmont, California: Wadsworth, Inc., 1986.

Bass, Bernard M. and Philip C. Burger. *Assessment of Managers: An International Comparison.* Free Press, 1979.

Condon, John and Fathi Yousef. *An Introduction to Intercultural Communication.* Bobbs-Merrill, 1974.

Davis, Stanley M. *Comparative Management: Organizational and Cultural Perspectives.* Englewood Cliffs, NJ: Prentice-Hall, 1971.

Glenn, Edmund. "Meaning and Behavior: Communication and Culture." *Journal of Communication,* December, 1966.

Graham, John. "Brazilian, Japanese and American Business Negotiations." *Journal of International Business Studies,* Spring–Summer, 1983, pp. 44–61.

Gulliver, P.H. *Disputes and Negotiations: A Cross-Cultural Perspective.* Academic, 1979.

Hall, Edward T. *Beyond Culture.* Garden City, NY: Anchor Press/ Doubleday, 1976.

———. *The Dance of Life: The Other Dimension of Time.* Garden City, NY: Anchor Press/Doubleday, 1983.

———. *The Hidden Dimension.* Garden City, NY: Anchor Press/Doubleday, 1966.

———. *The Silent Language.* Garden City, NY: Anchor Press/ Doubleday, 1959.

Henderson, George and Virginia Hall Milhouse. *International Business and Cultures.* New York: Cummings and Hathaway Publishers, 1987.

Hofstede, Geert. *Culture's Consequences.* Sage, 1984.

Lewis, Flora. *Europe: A Tapestry of Nations.* New York: Simon & Schuster, 1987.

Terpstra, Vern (ed.). *The Cultural Environment of International Business.* Cincinnati: Southwestern Publishing Company, 1978.

BIBLIOGRAPHY
International Business Negotiations

Binnendijk, Hanns. *National Negotiation Styles.* U.S. Department of State, Foreign Service Institute, 1987.

Cohen, Herb. *You Can Negotiate Anything.* Secaucus, NJ: Lyle Stuart, 1980.

Fayerweather, John and Ashook Kapoor. *Strategy and Negotiation for the International Corporation.* Ballinger, 1976.

Fisher, Glen. *International Negotiations: A Cross-Cultural Perspective.* Yarmouth, Maine: Intercultural Press, 1980.

Fisher, Roger and William Ury. *Getting to Yes.* Boston: Houghton Mifflin New York: Penguin, 1983.

Graham, John L. and Roy A. Herberger. "Negotiators Abroad—Don't Shoot from the Hip." *Harvard Business Review,* July/August 1983, pp. 160–168.

Harris, Philip R. and Robert T. Moran. *Managing Cultural Differences,* 3rd edition. Houston: Gulf Publishing Co., 1990.

Hofstede, Geert. *Culture's Consequences.* Sage, 1984.

Ikle, Fred C. *How Nations Negotiate.* Harper and Row, 1964.

Nierenberg, Gerard I. *The Complete Negotiator.* New York: Nierenberg & Zief Publishers, 1985.

Posses, Frederick. *The Art of International Negotiation.* London: Business Books, 1978.

Raiffa, Howard. *The Art and Science of Negotiation.* Harvard University Press. 1982.

Terpstra, Vern (ed.). *The Cultural Environment of International Business.* Cincinnati: Southwestern Publishing Co., 1978.

Triandis, Harry C. and William Wilson Lambert. *Handbook of Cross-Cultural Psychology.* Vols. 1–6. Boston: Allyn and Bacon, Inc., 1980.

Weiss, Stephen E. and William Stripp. *Negotiating With Foreign Businesspersons.* New York University Working Paper No. 1, February, 1985.

Index

....

G